GRATITUDE TO ALLAH

MARRIAGE 101

A Muslim's Guide to the Sacred Bond

FAITH PUBLICATIONS

All thanks are due to Allah *subhaanahu wa ta'ala* for enabling us with this effort.
Special thanks to the following contributors:

Content Writer: Sh. Sabri Benkahla
Islamic Studies Curriculum Editing Team: Amber Bokhari, Walida Mukhtar, Zara Tariq
Copy Editor: Amber Bokhari
Curriculum Coordinator: Samira Hingoro
Graphic and Layout Design: Farah Firman

A project of Dar-us-Salaam community, College Park, MD, USA
www.darussalaam.org

Printed in the United States of America

For permission requests, write to the publisher at the address below.

FAITH Publications
5301 Edgewood Road
College Park, MD 20740, USA
Phone: 301-982-9848
Email: iscurriculum@alhuda.org
faithpublications.org

TABLE OF CONTENTS

UNIT 1 | MARRIAGE: A SACRED BOND

UNIT 2 | MARRIAGE: THE START OF A NEW JOURNEY TOGETHER

PREFACE

Are you a teenager who is curious about marriage? Perhaps a young adult in the process of getting married? Maybe a middle-aged couple struggling in your 15-year marriage? Or possibly a confused spouse trying to make sense of your rights? Then you have selected the right book. In a world where the purpose and sacredness of marriage is constantly called into question, it becomes compulsory for Muslims to educate themselves about one of the greatest acts of worship, the scared bond. "Marriage 101: A Muslim's Guide to the Sacred Bond," defines and explores the rights, roles, and responsibilities of both spouses. Getting married completes half of your faith as a Muslim, yet many Muslims are ignorant about the various virtues, conditions, and approaches outlined in the *Qur'an* and the *Sunnah*. Entering a marriage contract without the understanding of your rights and the rights of your spouse can create a recipe for disaster.

It is essential for every Muslim to understand the purpose of marriage and its sacred status in Islam. From defining the virtues of marriage to dissecting the rights and responsibilities of both the husband and wife in a balanced approach, this book will provide you with the foundational knowledge of how to start and maintain a healthy Allah-centered marriage. Deriving the guidance from the *Qur'an* and the example of Prophet Muhammad *sallAllahu 'alayhi wa sallam*, these chapters will expand and alter the way you view marriage.

This book is the third Life Skills book which is a part of our Gratitude to Allah series. This series belongs to a new Islamic Studies curriculum; a curriculum which aims to help you apply your faith to real world issues. It presents every day, practical applications of Islam. We pray that this book helps you draw closer to Allah as you learn and apply the knowledge in this book to your daily life. Please send your feedback to iscurriculum@alhuda.org. We welcome any suggestions to improve this curriculum. Lastly, we would like to thank Sheikh Sabri BenKahla for writing the units so beautifully and sharing with us his wealth of knowledge and experience. May Allah accept this effort from him and everyone who worked on this book, and more importantly, may Allah accept your efforts to draw closer to Him.

UNIT 1

MARRIAGE: A SACRED BOND

UNIT 1

IMPORTANT VOCABULARY

AL-AHAD
The One, The Unique who is forever One and has never and will never have another alongside Him

AL-BASEER
The All-Seeing, The All-Perceiving, The All-Comprehending

AL-FIRDAWS
It is the highest level of Paradise

AL-KHAALIQ
The Creator, The One who brings everything from non-existence to existence

AMANAH Trust

AQEEQAH
The sacrifice of an animal on the occasion of the birth of a child

'AWRAH
The parts of the body which are considered private according to Islam and should be covered in the presence of others, such as chest to knee area for women, hair for women, navel to knee area for men, etc. However, the meaning of the word " *'awrah*" may vary based on the context and based on differences in schools of thoughts of Islamic jurisprudence.

BARAKAH Blessing

DEEN
Religion, the complete way of life worshipping Allah

GHALEEDH Firm and strong

HIKMAH Wisdom

IJAAB Affirmation

IJMAA'
Consensus of Scholars; is a unanimous agreement among the scholars of the ummah after the death of the Prophet *sallAllahu 'alayhi wa sallam* during any era on a particular matter

LIBAAS
Clothing or garment

MAHR
Dowry; an obligatory gift from the groom to the bride

MAHRAM
Referring to a husband, wife, or a family member with whom marriage is not allowed

MITHAAQAN GHALEEDHAA
A firm commitment, a firm covenant; referring to marriage

MITHAQ
Commitment, covenant

NASHEED
Islamic songs sung by voice only

NIKAAH
Marriage, Marriage contract

UMMAH
The whole community of Muslims

RIZQ Provision

SADAQAH
Refers to a voluntary deed or an act of kindness done sincerely for Allah. It is derived from the root word that means being true or sincere.

SALAAT-UL-ISTIKHAARAH
Prayer of seeking counsel; A prayer performed by those who are in need of guidance from Allah when facing a major decision in their lives.

TAWFIQ
A gift of opportunity, aid, and blessing from Allah

TAQWA
A protective barrier between you and Allah's punishment by acting on His commands and staying away from His prohibitions

WALI
Male guardian of the bride

WALIMAH
The wedding ceremony; the wedding feast

QABOOL Acceptance

TABLE OF CONTENTS

UNIT 1 | MARRIAGE: A SACRED BOND

ESSENTIAL QUESTIONS

This unit is designed to help answer the following questions.

1. How does marriage impact society?
2. Why is it important to know the goal of marriage in Islam?
3. How do you get married in Islam?
4. Why is it necessary to have a *wali*?

CHAPTER 1

MARRIAGE IN ISLAM

Marriage in Islam is only between a man and a woman. It is considered a legal union that protects society from moral degradation. [1] Marriage allows a man and a woman to live together in love and happiness, and to create a safe atmosphere to raise a family.

The Purpose of Marriage: Is Marriage Just for Love?

The goal of marriage isn't just for love, but it is to fulfill our natural instincts in a manner ordained by Allah that will contribute to our betterment and the betterment of society. It is a blessed way to have a companion in our lives to help us work through various ups and downs in this world and help us strive together to draw closer to Allah.

One of the main purposes of marriage is to grow the bonds between the husband and wife which are the foundation of a family and a pillar of society. Marriage provides stability to the spouses and is a means to increase love, mercy, and understanding between them and the world at large. Matrimony is the only legitimate path to children, family, and a flourishing society.

1. Moral degradation involves a society's progressive loss of or weakening of the moral and ethical standards that prevailed in the social traditions.

Importance of Marriage in the *Qur'an*

The institution of marriage is one of the greatest gifts Allah has given to humanity. In fact, Allah has described it as one of His signs. Allah says,

وَمِنْ ءَايَـٰتِهِۦٓ أَنْ خَلَقَ لَكُم مِّنْ أَنفُسِكُمْ أَزْوَٰجًا
لِّتَسْكُنُوٓا۟ إِلَيْهَا وَجَعَلَ بَيْنَكُم مَّوَدَّةً وَرَحْمَةً ۚ إِنَّ فِى
ذَٰلِكَ لَـَٔايَـٰتٍ لِّقَوْمٍ يَتَفَكَّرُونَ

"And of His signs is that He created for you from yourselves mates that you may find tranquility in them, and He placed between you affection and mercy. Indeed in that are signs for a people who give thought." [2]

Marriage is considered a milestone and one of the biggest events in our lives. Allah described it as ***Mithaaqan Ghaleedhaa*** (a firm commitment). Allah says,

وَكَيْفَ تَأْخُذُونَهُۥ وَقَدْ أَفْضَىٰ بَعْضُكُمْ إِلَىٰ بَعْضٍ
وَأَخَذْنَ مِنكُم مِّيثَـٰقًا غَلِيظًا

*"And how could you take it back after having enjoyed each other intimately and she has taken from you a **firm commitment**?"* [3]

Mithaaq means commitment or covenant, and the word ***ghaleedh*** means firm and strong. When you say a garment is *ghaleedh* it means that you cannot tear through it,

---

2. Surah Ar-Rum [30:21]
3. Surah An-NIsaa' [4:21]

cut it, or shred it, as it is built extremely strong. The marriage and the contract itself are both like this: a firm commitment and covenant.

We go from being single to becoming life partners. We merge two separate families into one to create a whole new family. Since marriage is such a great endeavor and an institution ordained by Allah, it is only befitting that we should be guided by the *Qur'an* and the *Sunnah* every step of the way. It is important that we begin our journey of marriage with the mindset that we want to complete our religion and please Allah. From finding a spouse, to getting to know the spouse, to the engagement, the marriage contract, the marriage celebration, and life after the marriage celebration, we must always keep in mind that Allah is ***Al-Baseer*** (The All-Seeing). We have the ultimate marriage handbook in the book of Allah and the *Sunnah* of His messenger *sallAllahu 'alayhi wa sallam*, so we should use them as our guides.

WHAT IS A FIRM COMMITMENT

It is the promise of a solid commitment to one another as husband and wife when agreeing to marry. It is the only contract (commitment) in the *Qur'an* for which Allah used the adjective *ghaleedh* (a firm commitment). It is described as such because of how solid, strong, powerful, and close the relationship between husband and wife should be and how important the rights and obligations each have towards one another are.

4. Surah Ar-Ra'ad [13:38]

Importance of Marriage in the Sunnah

Marriage is highly encouraged in Islam because it is the *sunnah* of the prophets and messengers. Allah says,

وَلَقَدْ أَرْسَلْنَا رُسُلًا مِّن قَبْلِكَ وَجَعَلْنَا لَهُمْ أَزْوَاجًا وَذُرِّيَّةً ۚ

"And We have already sent messengers before you and made for them wives and descendants" [4]

A marriage will thrive when we follow the sunnah of marrying. A righteous family will always contribute to building a strong community and society. The Prophet *sallAllahu 'alayhi wa sallam* further stressed the importance of marriage when he *sallAllahu 'alayhi wa sallam* said,

"Marriage is part of my sunnah, and whoever does not follow my sunnah has nothing to do with me. Get married, for I will boast of your great numbers before the nations. Whoever has the means, let him get married, and whoever does not, then he should fast for it will diminish his desire." [5]

Completion of Faith

Marriage is also a means to complete and enhance our faith and character. The Prophet *sallAllahu 'alayhi wa sallam* said,
"When someone marries they have completed half of their religion..." [6]

Marriage plays a huge role in protecting someone from following their desires, helps one to lower their gaze, fulfills many of our fundamental needs, and it is the basis in which we build our lives and society. Thus, we have completed half of our religion just by marrying. In another narration, the Prophet *sallAllahu 'alayhi wa sallam* said,

"When a person gets married he has completed half of his religion, so let him fear Allah with regard to the other half." [7]

---

5. Ibn Majah
6. Al-Bayhaqi
7. Al-Bayhaqi

BRAIN TEASER

Why do you really want to get Married?

Marriage is a lifelong union that needs to be thoroughly thought out. Just like we plan out our weddings in so much detail, we must plan out which direction we want our marriage to head towards. When you see yourself marrying, how do you hope your future marriage *In shaa Allah* will add to your life and what do you want to accomplish by getting married?

CHAPTER 2

WHY MARRY?

Through the institution of marriage, procreation occurs in a manner that protects the rights of the husband, wife, children, and society at large. The wisdom of marriage is profound. Some of its benefits and pearls of wisdom are discussed below.

1 MARRIAGE IS A BLESSING

Marriage is a blessing and a way for us to learn about compassion, love, and mercy. Allah in His ***Hikmah*** (wisdom) has chosen to make His creation in pairs. He is ***Al-Ahad*** (The One) and needs no partner or offspring. But as human beings, we are social creatures and need companionship. He has chosen to bless every soul with a mate which will be found in this world for those who marry and in the *akhirah* for those who were unable to do so in this life. Allah tells us,

هُوَ ٱلَّذِى خَلَقَكُم مِّن نَّفْسٍ وَٰحِدَةٍ وَجَعَلَ مِنْهَا
زَوْجَهَا لِيَسْكُنَ إِلَيْهَا

"It is He who created you from one soul and created from it its mate that he might dwell in security with her." [8]

2 MARRIAGE HELPS RAISE RIGHTEOUS CHILDREN

Islamically, one of the wisdoms of marriage is to increase the population of Muslims by raising children who will worship Allah and share this beautiful way of life, Islam, with others. The Prophet *sallAllahu 'alayhi wa sallam* said,

"Marry, for I will boast of your great numbers." [9]

3 MARRIAGE HELPS DEVELOP SELF CONTROL

Marriage is also a means for men and women to control their desires. Allah does not prohibit anything except that He gives us a better alternative. Unlike in some religions where it is encouraged to ignore or suppress one's urges and instincts in order to be pious, Islam recognizes that there is a natural desire to be in an intimate physical relationship and has given us marriage as an outlet to fulfill those desires in a ***halal*** (permissible) manner that will also be rewarded. The Prophet *sallAllahu 'alayhi wa sallam* said,

"... and enjoining good is a sadaqah, and forbidding that which is evil is a sadaqah, and in man's intimacy there is a sadaqah. They (the companions) said: Messenger of Allah, is there reward for him who satisfies his desires among us? He said: Tell me, if he were to devote it to something forbidden, would it not be a sin on his part? Similarly, if he were to devote it to something lawful, he should have a reward." [10]

4 MARRIAGE PROVIDES PROTECTION, TRUE LOVE, AND COMFORT

Since marriage is a source of protection from many evils such as impermissible relationships (i.e. like having a boyfriend/girlfriend and having an inappropriate romantic relationship (such as fornication) before marriage). The Prophet *sallAllahu 'alayhi wa sallam* described the concept of true love being expressed through marriage. He *sallAllahu 'alayhi wa sallam* said,

"There is nothing like marriage, for two who love one another." [11]

---

8. Surah Al-'Araf [7:189]
9. Ibn Majah
10. Sahih Muslim

Additionally a person marries to find comfort and closeness within the spouse. Allah describes the nature of the closeness between the husband and wife as ***libaas*** (clothing). Allah says,

هُنَّ لِبَاسٌ لَّكُمْ وَأَنتُمْ لِبَاسٌ لَّهُنَّ

"They are clothing for you and you are clothing (tranquility, rest) for them." [12]

The analogy of spouses being *"clothing for you and you are clothing for them"* implies such a closeness that nothing should come between the spouses. It also expresses how intimate the relationship between a husband and a wife should be. Spouses are like garments to each other which protect, cover, comfort, and also bring out the best in each other.

WHAT DOES IT MEAN TO RESPECT A WOMAN?

Is respect shown by standing up when she walks into the room, by opening the door of a car for her, or is it something much deeper than this?

In today's society, we see the exploitation of women's dignity, honor, and body in many cultures, despite the widespread cries for women's rights across the world. Rather than seeing positive change, we see the use of images of women's bodies in various marketing campaigns, demeaning their intelligence and character as human beings.

Islam truly empowers the woman and respects a woman first and foremost for her character, her intelligence, and her commitment to Allah.

11. Ibn Majah
12. Surah Al-Baqarah [2:187]

5 MARRIAGE HELPS THE SOCIETY TO THRIVE

Marriage is the foundation of society as a whole. Every relationship stems from the husband and wife's relationship, and those relationships thrive best when the father and mother are bonded together by marriage. A strong Muslim couple who makes Allah and His Prophet *sallAllahu 'alayhi wa sallam* their main focus will know that life doesn't revolve solely around their own marriage, but that their family's strength and *iman* play a great role in building the Muslim community and developing a strong Islamic society for generations to come. If there was no institution of marriage, how could the continuity of a nation that worships Allah carry on? Some scholars say that the spiritual destruction of a person is caused by two things: the tongue and the private parts. As the Prophet *sallAllahu 'alayhi wa sallam* said,

"Whoever guarantees me (the chastity of) what is between his legs (i.e. his private parts), and what is between his jaws (i.e., his tongue), I guarantee him Paradise." [13]

DID YOU KNOW?

In the studies of fiqh there are five Islamic rulings:

1. **Wajib** (Obligatory)
2. **Mustahab** (Preferred)
3. **Mubah** (Permitted)
4. **Makrooh** (Disliked)
5. **Muharam** (Forbidden)

Marriage is so important that some scholars consider it *wajib*, a religious obligation. However, the majority of scholars say that marriage is *mustahab*, a *sunnah*, unless one fears falling into *haram*. Then, it becomes an obligation (*wajib*) upon him or her to marry.

13. Sahih Al-Bukhari

What if Someone Wants to Marry But is Unable to?

If a person is not able to get married for one reason or another, a person should stay patient, continue to make *du'aa* to Allah to solve their situation, and practice self control through fasting. The Prophet *sallAllahu 'alayhi wa sallam* advised us,

"O young people! Whoever among you can marry, should marry, because it helps him lower his gaze and guard his modesty (i.e. his private parts from committing illegal sexual intercourse etc.), and whoever is not able to marry, should fast, as fasting diminishes his sexual power."

Additionally, we should stay away from those situations that will lead us to temptations and where the boundaries of Allah are not respected. We should stay away from watching or listening to things that will increase our desires. Instead, we should keep ourselves occupied with actions which are beneficial. Keeping good company is another means to help protect ourselves. Allah tells us,

يَـٰٓأَيُّهَا ٱلَّذِينَ ءَامَنُوا۟ ٱتَّقُوا۟ ٱللَّهَ وَكُونُوا۟ مَعَ ٱلصَّـٰدِقِينَ

"O you who believe! Fear Allah, and stand with those who are truthful." [15]

The Prophet *sallAllahu 'alayhi wa sallam* informed us,

"A man follows the religion of his friend; so each one should consider whom he makes his friend." [16]

When you surround yourself with righteous friends, it will motivate you to be better. Another way to protect yourself if you can't get married is by coming closer to Allah with patience and strengthening your *salaah.* Allah says,

وَٱسْتَعِينُوا۟ بِٱلصَّبْرِ وَٱلصَّلَوٰةِ

"Seek assistance through patience and prayer..." [17]

14. Sahih Al-Bukhari
15. Surah At-Tawbah [9:119]
16. Abu Dawood
17. Surah Al-Baqarah [2:45]

WAYS TO SPEND OUR TIME WISELY

Being patient until you find the right one can be in the form of utilizing your time wisely. The more you keep yourself busy with beneficial things, the more your mind won't dwell into prohibited things. As the saying goes: *"Idleness is the devil's playground,"* or *"An idle mind is the devil's workshop."* Being idle and not using our gift of time wisely is one of the ways *shaytaan* is able to get to us.

Some ways to keep busy are:

EXCERCISE WITH A FRIEND

LEARN A NEW SKILL OR TRADE THAT WILL BE HELPFUL TO YOU

JOIN A WEEKLY ISLAMIC GATHERING

WORK TOWARDS MEMORIZING THE *QUR'AN*

VOLUNTEER WITH A CHARITABLE ORGANIZATION

PARTICIPATE & ORGANIZE EVENTS TO BENEFIT OTHERS

CHAPTER 1 & 2

REVIEW AND REFLECT QUESTIONS

1

The Prophet *sallAllahu 'alayhi wa sallam* said, *"A person is upon the religion of his best friend, so let one of you look at whom he befriends."* [18] This *hadith* is specific on how we choose our best friends, but how does this *hadith* apply even more when choosing a spouse?

2

Explain two ways a successful marriage can impact other lives within the community.

3

In your opinion, what are the pros and cons of getting married at a young age?

4

What do you think would happen to society if there was no institution of marriage?

5

Ahmed wants to get married but doesn't have the financial means to do so. He decides that looking at women's pictures online will help control his desires. Is his method correct? Why or why not? What advice would you give him?

CHAPTER 3

CHOOSING A SPOUSE

Like many choices in life, choosing a spouse is a decision you do not want to take lightly. Who you choose will have a great impact upon your happiness, your emotional and physical well-being, and it will also influence how you will raise your family. The Prophet *sallAllahu 'alayhi wa sallam* said,

"A woman is married for four things; her wealth, her family status, her beauty and her religion. So you should marry the religious woman (otherwise) you will be a loser." [19]

So we can see that ***deen*** (religion) and ***taqwa*** (piety) should be the top priority when choosing a spouse. When looking for a potential spouse, think about whether you would be happy with this person becoming the father or mother of your child. If you were to pass away, would you feel comfortable with this person taking care of raising your family?

19. Sahih Al-Bukhari

DU'AA FOR A RIGHTEOUS SPOUSE

Sometimes, no matter how much we do our due diligence or think we know a person before marriage, we may end up with the wrong spouse. That doesn't mean we should not do our due diligence, but we should make sure to couple it with *du'aa*. Only Allah knows the hearts and the character of each individual. Making *du'aa* increases your chances that Allah will bring the person in your life who will be good for you. In Islam, we are highly encouraged to make *du'aa* for a spouse and offspring. Allah tells us,

وَٱلَّذِينَ يَقُولُونَ رَبَّنَا هَبْ لَنَا مِنْ أَزْوَٰجِنَا وَذُرِّيَّٰتِنَا قُرَّةَ أَعْيُنٍ وَٱجْعَلْنَا لِلْمُتَّقِينَ إِمَامًا

"And those who say, 'Our Lord, grant us from among our wives and offspring comfort to our eyes and make us a leader for the righteous.'" [20]

---

20. Surah Al-Furqan [25:74]

THE IMPACT OF CHOOSING **THE RIGHT SPOUSE**

The impact of choosing the right spouse with the right criteria in mind has a far reaching effect. It doesn't only affect you, but it also affects the lives of your children and others around you. Its impact is highlighted by a story from our history.

Once a man came to 'Umar [21] *radhiAllahu 'anhu* complaining about his son's disobedience to him. 'Umar *radhiAllahu 'anhu* called for the boy and spoke of his disobedience to his father and his neglect of his rights. The boy replied:

"O Ameer Al-Mu'mineen (Leader of the Believers)! Hasn't a child rights over his father?" "Certainly", replied 'Umar *radhiAllahu 'anhu*. *"What are they, Ameer Al-Mu'mineen?" "That he should choose his mother, give him a good name and teach him the Book (the Qur'an)." "O Ameer Al-Mu'mineen! My father did nothing of this. My mother was a Magian (fire worshipper). He gave me the name of Julalan (meaning dung beetle or scarab) and he did not teach me a single letter of the Qur'an."* Turning to the father, 'Umar *radhiAllahu 'anhu* said: *"You have come to me to complain about the disobedience of your son. You have failed in your duty to him before he has failed in his duty to you; you have done wrong to him before he has wronged you."* [22]

We can see here that 'Umar *radhiAllahu 'anhu* held the father accountable for his son's disobedience because of the spouse he chose and how he had neglected his son's upbringing and care in the light of the book of Allah. The foundation of your child's upbringing begins before birth with the selection of a spouse.

21. Famous Companion of the Prophet *sallAllahu 'alayhi wa sallam* and 2nd Khalifah (leader) of the Muslims.
22. Story related by Ibn Al-Jawzy *rahimahullaah*

Common Steps Towards Finding a Spouse [23]

1 DU'AA

Make *du'aa* to Allah that He provides you with a righteous spouse that will be the comfort of your eyes and help you in your worldly and religious affairs. Allah says,

وَٱلَّذِينَ يَقُولُونَ رَبَّنَا هَبْ لَنَا مِنْ أَزْوَٰجِنَا
وَذُرِّيَّٰتِنَا قُرَّةَ أَعْيُنٍ وَٱجْعَلْنَا لِلْمُتَّقِينَ إِمَامًا

"And those who say, "Our Lord, grant us from among our wives and offspring comfort to our eyes and make us an example for the righteous." [24]

The Prophet *sallAllahu 'alayhi wa sallam* said,

"Let one of you ask his Lord for his needs, all of them, even for a shoestring when his breaks." [25]

2 CHECK YOUR INTENTION

Why do you want to get married? This question is very important because it will form the foundation of who you are looking for as well. As a Muslim, marriage shouldn't just be about fulfilling our desires or marrying for superficial reasons such as all my friends are getting married and I need to marry someone too. Instead, it should be about building a family and finding a companion that will help take you to *Jannah*. Before you can find a spouse, you should have a deeper understanding of yourself and your priorities in life. What are your views and life perspectives? What do you expect from marriage?

---

23. Adapted from the article "Is Passionate Love in Marriage...Real?" by Maryam Amirebrahimi
24. Surah Al-Furqan [25:74]
25. At-Tirmidhi

Are there any particular needs you seek in a relationship? Also, keep in mind marriage is not going to solve all your own personal problems. Yes, marriage is a support, and if we pick the right spouse, it will help us to be better individuals. But it is not fair to the spouse to expect them to be a solution to problems you have developed on your own. Every Muslim should be working on themselves before marriage so that they can be ready to be good partners and lift one another up as opposed to weighing each other down.

3 YOUR IDEAL SPOUSE

What do you want in a spouse? Religious belief should be top of your list and the most important quality you seek in a spouse. As mentioned earlier, the Prophet *sallAllahu 'alayhi wa sallam* said,

"A woman is married for four things; her wealth, her family status, her beauty and her religion. So you should marry the religious woman (otherwise) you will be a loser." [26]

Additionally, you should also form a list of criteria that you personally would want in your future spouse. Write down the qualities that you consider a must, qualities that you prefer, qualities that you dislike, and qualities that are an absolute deal breaker for you. This list is not set in stone and can always be changed, but it is a good starting point for you to pinpoint exactly what you want in your spouse.

4 GET SOMEONE INVOLVED

Engage intermediaries: [27]

To prevent embarrassment, improper relationships, uncomfortable situations and heartache, you should get someone reliable involved in the process. Sometimes it is best to go through someone else to find out if the person you are interested in might be interested in you without them knowing who you are. If you

26. Sahih Al-Bukhari

27. A person who acts as a link between people in order to try and bring about an agreement; a mediator.

want to communicate directly with the person, you must have someone reliable involved, whether it be a parent or a reliable chaperone with you. The Prophet *sallAllahu 'alayhi wa sallam* said,

"Not one of you should meet a woman alone unless she is accompanied by a relative within the prohibited degrees." [28]

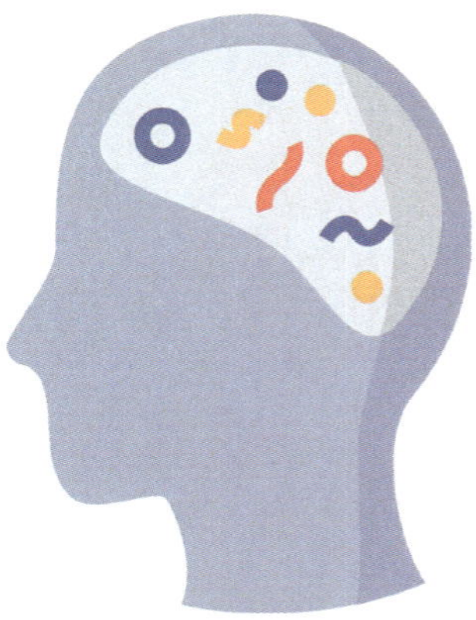

5 MIND FIRST

Engage your mind before your heart. Sometimes, it is easy to allow the excitement of marriage to influence our emotions, but this could have dangerous consequences. The romantic idea of falling in love before marriage is not in line with our Islamic belief system, and many times this idea of love is just an infatuation. Of course, we are emotional beings and emotions are perfectly fine in the right context. But before marriage, we should not be blinded by them to the point where we ignore logic. Many times a couple will be caught up in emotions and the excitement of having a relationship for the first time only to be disappointed after marrying because they chose to ignore red flags. It is very important to use your mind logically before getting involved emotionally. This will prevent a lot of heartaches and headaches. If someone gets emotionally attached and it doesn't work out, they are heartbroken.

However, being wise and making sure you are compatible first will prevent this. 'Umar ibn Al-Khattab *radhiAllahu 'anhu* said upon the pulpit,

"Verily, if a servant humbles himself for Allah Almighty, he will increase his wisdom." [29]

28. Sahih Al-Bukhari and Sahih Muslim
29. Ibn Hajar

X WATCH OUT X

FOR THIS RED FLAG!

An area of concern is when the spouse-to-be does not want his or her marriage to be recorded legally in their local jurisdiction. By not having a marriage recorded legally, you do not have any legal protection if things don't work out after marriage (i.e. divorce), especially living in a non-Muslim society. Make sure to have a conversation about this topic with your spouse-to-be and this subject should never be taken lightly.

6 PRAY SALAAT-UL-ISTIKHAARAH

If you think you found someone that might fit your criteria, seek Allah's help. The first thing any Muslim should do upon making any major decision like marriage is to seek assistance from Allah and pray *salaat-ul-istikharaah* (prayer of seeking counsel) [30]. Ibn Taymiyah [31] *rahimahullaah* used to say, *"He will never regret it who prays istikhaarahh seeking the guidance of the Creator and who seeks advice from people, then remains steadfast in whatever decision he makes."* [32]

7 SEEK ADVICE

A Muslim should always be keen to learn and seek advice before endeavoring into something. This is indeed a sign of a person's wisdom. Seeking guidance should be with an adult who you trust completely who will protect your privacy or from professional counselors who have experience in the field of Islamic marriage. Allah says,

فَسْـَٔلُوٓا۟ أَهْلَ ٱلذِّكْرِ إِن كُنتُمْ لَا تَعْلَمُونَ

"...So ask the people of the knowledge if you do not know." [33]

---

30. Refer to the appendix to learn more on how to perform this prayer.
31. Famous Scholar of *hadith, tafsir,* and *fiqh* (d.1328AD)
32. Al-Waabil As-Sayyib by Ibn Qayyim Al-Jawziyyah
33. Surah An-Nahl [16:43]

DID YOU KNOW?

How do you know the answer to your *salaat-ul-istikharaah?* If you make a decision after making *salaat-ul-istikharaah* and the the decision is good for you, everything will occur easily and smoothly. If you find out something negative about the person or you face many obstacles, then know that decision is not good for you. *Many people hope they will see a dream as an answer to *salaat-ul-istikharaah*. However, in Islam, dreams solely cannot be used to make life decisions. In Islam, whether it be in worship or worldly affairs, everything is guided by the *Qur'an* and the *Sunnah*.

BRAIN TEASER

The Messenger of Allah *sallAllahu 'alayhi wa sallam* said,

"Paradise has one hundred levels, and between every two levels is a distance like that between the heavens and earth. ***Al-Firdaws*** *is its highest level, from which four rivers of Paradise flow, and above is the Throne.* ***When you ask from Allah, ask for Al-Firdaws."*** [34]

The Prophet *sallAllahu 'alayhi wa sallam* guided us in this *hadith* to ask for the best, and in this case, *Al-Firdaws* is the highest level of *Jannah*. If we look at what we want in a spouse, we should be making *du'aa* to Allah for the best in our future spouse. What does the *'best spouse'* mean to you? In what way(s) will you improve your *du'aa* in regards to asking Allah to grant you your ideal future spouse?

34. At-Tirmidhi

CHAPTER 4

THE PROCESS OF MARRIAGE

In Islam, whether it be in worship or worldly affairs everything is guided by the *Qur'an* and the *Sunnah*. Just as we need to know the rituals of *salaah*, fasting, *zakaah*, and *hajj* to worship Allah correctly, we also need to learn about the correct process of getting married according to Islam. Additionally, we need to clear up some of the myths and folklore which have seeped around marriage into our traditions and cultures, and that will help us prepare for marriage with the right footing and pleasure of Allah. Let's take a look at the process of marriage in Islam after you have found a suitable potential spouse.

1. **ENGAGEMENT:** The declaration of the intention of marriage
2. **NIKAAH**: The actual marriage contract
3. **WALIMAH:** The wedding celebration after the marriage

Engagements In Islam

Prior to the actual marriage, there is usually the period of engagement. In Islam, engagement is not the same as in other religions or cultures in which they treat the engaged individuals as actual married partners. Islamically, engagement is simply the expression or declaration of the intention of marriage. It is not marriage itself.

How Does The Engagement Occur?

The engagement occurs by the man going to the *wali* and asking for the daughter's hand in marriage. Marriage can be proposed by either the man or the woman, but it is usually the case that the man proposes to the *wali*. It is very important to get the *wali* involved from the beginning so no impropriety occurs and the woman's reputation is held intact. There are many engagements that occur improperly, and they almost always end in failure with someone getting hurt. *Alhamdulilah,* Islam always seeks to protect all individuals, so there are boundaries we should adhere to.

What Should You Do During The Engagement?

Since engagement is not the actual marriage, one should adhere to the following etiquettes during engagements. Respecting these guidelines ensures Allah's pleasure and His blessings which are so badly needed when you embark on this new chapter in life.

It is not permitted to offer a proposal of marriage to the bride-to-be if she is already engaged (since she and her *wali* have already accepted someone else's proposal). An engaged couple is not permitted to be in each other's company (or act) as married couples do. Hence, they cannot be alone together until the *nikaah* is performed. During the engagement period, they should still deal with each other similar to how one deals with anyone of the opposite gender. The Prophet *sallAllahu 'alayhi wa sallam* reminded us,

"No man is alone with a woman, except that their third party is the shaytaan." [35]

However, there should be facilitation for the engaged parties to speak to one another to see if they are compatible within the bounds of proper etiquette. This should always be done with the permission of the *wali,* preferably under his supervision, or in a public avenue in the company of other relatives.

---

35. Sahih Al-Bukhari and Sahih Muslim

DID YOU KNOW?

One should not propose to a woman whose family has already accepted another proposal.

However, there is a difference of opinion on this issue. [36] If the family has accepted the proposal and is keen on moving forward, no other proposal should be put forward. The Prophet *sallAllahu 'alayhi wa sallam* said,

"A man should not propose to a woman his brother has proposed to, nor should he undercut his brother in business transactions." [37]

However, if the woman hasn't made a decision yet and is unsure about the first proposal, it is permissible. This is according to the ***hadith*** of Fatima bint Qais [38] *radhiAllahu 'anha* when she went to the Prophet *sallAllahu 'alayhi wa sallam* and told him that Muawiyah, Abu Jahm, and Osama bin Zaid [39] *radhiAllahu 'anhum* all asked for her hand in marriage. The Prophet *sallAllahu 'alayhi wa sallam* said,

"Muawiyah has no wealth, Abu Jahm is abusive towards women, so I advise you with Osama. She raised her hands in amusement and asked Osama?! The Prophet sallAllahu 'alayhi wa sallam said obedience to Allah and obedience to the messenger is better for you so she married Osama. And she said after marrying Osama that she was so happy and blessed in her decision and that she became the envy [40] of other women..." [41]

---

36. We have listed the strongest opinion amongst the scholars regarding this issue.
37. Sahih Al-Bukhari and Sahih Muslim
38. Female companion of the Prophet *sallAllahu 'alayhid wa sallam.*
39. Famous companions at the time of the Prophet *sallAllahu 'alayhi wa sallam*
40. In this case, what is meant by envy is ghibtah, which is good envy, where a person has the desire to achieve the good qualities that others have. But it is free from malice or wanting the blessing they see to be taken away from the person.
41. Sahih Al-Bukhari

What Is Nikaah? (Marriage)

Nikaah literally means to unite and come together. In Islam it is the joining of two separate individuals through marriage. *Nikaah* is considered a binding contract that makes it permissible for a man and woman to be intimate with each other. *Nikaah* is legislated by Allah in the *Qur'an,* the *Sunnah* of the Prophet *sallAllahu 'alayhi wa sallam,* and *Ijmaa'* (consensus of scholars). [42]

What is Included in The Nikaah?

1. **A Marriage contract**
   - An offer from the ***wali*** (male guardian)
   - An acceptance from the groom
2. **An agreed-upon *mahr* (dowry) to be given to the bride**
3. **Witnesses**

   We will discuss each of these essential components of the *nikaah* in detail later in this book.

1 NIKAAH IN THE *QUR'AN*

Allah tells us in the *Qur'an,*

فَٱنكِحُواْ مَا طَابَ لَكُم مِّنَ ٱلنِّسَآءِ

"... then marry those that please you of women..." [43]

In another verse Allah says,

وَأَنكِحُواْ ٱلۡأَيَـٰمَىٰ مِنكُمۡ وَٱلصَّـٰلِحِينَ مِنۡ عِبَادِكُمۡ وَإِمَآئِكُمۡ

"And marry the unmarried among you and the righteous among your male slaves and female slaves..." [44]

42. Consensus of the Scholars
43. Surah An-Nisaa' [4:3]
44. Surah An-Nur [24:32]

2 NIKAAH IN THE SUNNAH

The Prophet *sallAllahu 'alayhi wa sallam* said, *"Marriage is part of my sunnah, and whoever does not follow my sunnah has nothing to do with me. Get married, for I will boast of your great numbers before the nations. Whoever has the means, let him get married, and whoever does not, then he should fast for it will diminish his desire."* [45]

As narrated by Abdullah Ibn Mas'ud [46] *radhiAllahu 'anhu: "We were with the Prophet sallAllahu 'alayhi wa sallam while we were young and had no wealth. So Allah's Messenger sallAllahu 'alayhi wa sallam said,*

"O young people! Whoever among you can marry, should marry because it helps him lower his gaze and guard his modesty, and whoever is not able to marry, should fast, as fasting diminishes his desires." [47]

3 NIKAAH IS AGREED UPON BY IJMAA' (CONSENSUS OF SCHOLARS)

Ijmaa' is a unanimous agreement among the scholars of Islam after the death of the Prophet *sallAllahu 'alayhi wa sallam* during any era on a particular matter. The scholars of the Muslim *ummah* have unanimously agreed that marriage is a part of Islam.

45. Ibn Majah
46. A famous companion of the Prophet *sallAllahu 'alayhi wa sallam*, expert in *Tafsir* and prominent transmitter of *hadith*.
47. Sahih Al-Bukhari

WHO YOU ARE NOT ALLOWED TO MARRY?

- X A polytheist.
- X Relatives that are your mahram. [48]
- X A Muslim woman cannot marry a non-Muslim man.
- X A man cannot marry two sisters at the same time or an aunt and niece at the same time.
- X One cannot marry the exes of one's parents or the exes of one's children.
- X One cannot marry the parents or children of someone that they have been previously married to.
- X Marrying the same gender. [49]

48. A person with whom marriage is prohibited due to their close blood relationship, or due to being breastfed, or due to a relation through marriage. See Surah An-Nur [22-24] for a comprehensive list of the people who one is not allowed to marry.
49. Marriage in Islam is only between a biological man and a biological woman.

Just Married

WHY **MUSLIM MEN** ARE **ALLOWED TO MARRY** (CHASTE, PRACTICING) CHRISTIAN & JEWISH WOMEN AND **MUSLIM WOMEN ARE NOT?**

In order to understand this, we must understand what are the pre-conditions for a Muslim man to be allowed to marry a Jewish or Christian woman are:

She should be a chaste woman (someone who has not had physical relations with any man outside of marriage).

She should be a practicing (Jewish or Christian) woman who adheres to her scriptures, not someone who claims to be Jewish or Christian but ascribes herself to a secular, atheistic mindset.

This allowance for Muslim men is generally given in a context of a Muslim society. Scholars discourage Muslim men living in a non-Muslim society to marry non-Muslim women because of the potential religious influence upon their children and also to ensure that Muslim women can be married.

WHY **MUSLIM WOMEN ARE NOT ALLOWED** TO MARRY NON- MUSLIM MEN?

When it comes to why Muslim women are not allowed to marry a Jewish or Christian man, first and foremost it is because Allah in His wisdom did not allow Muslim women to be married to a non-Muslim. We know that Allah is All-Wise and All-Just and that He knows us better than we know ourselves. So, when Allah has legislated this law, it is a matter of what will work best for Muslim women and fulfill the goal of marriage for her.

The role and responsibility of a husband in Islam is to lead the family and provide spiritual guidance. In order to lead the family and provide spiritual guidance, one needs to believe in Allah, His prophet *sallAllahu ‘alayhi wa sallam*, and the message of Islam. Someone who does not believe in Islam will not be able to help the family and nurture their spiritual growth. Also, one of the responsibilities of a Muslim wife in Islam is to listen to, respect, and obey her husband as long as He doesn’t go against the teachings of Allah and His messenger *sallAllahu ‘alayhi wa sallam*. A wife is not allowed to listen to, respect, and obey a husband if his decisions in life are contrary to Islam. So how can she fulfill these rights if the premise of the husband’s belief is against Islam? When the basic religious beliefs of a husband and wife do not align, there will be constant marital discord and stress in a marriage. The wife may have to compromise on her own principles and beliefs to maintain peace in the house. There will be no accountability or mutual set of values which can be upheld if the husband falters.

And what will happen to the children? If the husband is the authority of the household, the children will most likely follow in his footsteps. These may be some of the wisdoms behind the prohibition of a Muslim woman marrying a non-Muslim man.

CHAPTER 3 & 4

REVIEW AND REFLECT QUESTIONS

1

Fatima got engaged last summer and was planning to marry the following year. She and her fiancé would meet once a week in a public venue to get to know each other without her parents' approval. They became so comfortable with each other that the initial shyness they both had disappeared. Fatima couldn't wait to get married, but her fiancé began having doubts. He spent every week with Fatima for over 7 months and he feels he doesn't want to commit to the marriage anymore. So, he breaks off the engagement. What mistakes do you see occurring in this scenario and how could have they been avoided?

2

Mona is looking to get married, and she is interested in a boy named Talha who she has seen involved in different events at her *masjid*. What are the proper steps she should take to learn more about Talha and whether he would be a good fit for her or not?

3

Name two reasons why we should always have a responsible intermediary involved when seeking out a spouse.

4

What are the benefits of choosing to marry a righteous spouse over someone who is not so righteous?

5

When we like someone, we tend to overlook the red flags. Red flags are warning signs that may indicate unhealthy behavior. What are some red flags that you may look out for in a potential spouse? Explain what makes these qualities red flags. Why is it important to not ignore the red flags when we are searching for a spouse?

BEFORE YOU MARRY

What Is The Proper Way To Know Someone?

If you have the sincere intention to marry someone, it is permissible to find out more about them by observing them without them knowing. Sometimes people tend to be on their best behavior and act more polite when people are watching them, but this may not be their normal behavior. The purpose of observing the person is to see how he or she interacts with others, to assess their true character, and most importantly to see if there is compatibility. Without being intrusive or invasive, observing the person should also help you find out if there is an attraction that would

make you want to marry them. The Prophet *sallAllahu 'alayhi wa sallam* said,

"If one of you proposes marriage to a woman, if he can look at her to see that which will encourage him to go ahead and marry her, then let him do so." [50]

Compatibility

Compatibility is vital for a healthy and satisfying marriage. Compatibility refers to the ability for two individuals to live harmoniously while respecting each other's differences. It is very important to make sure you are compatible from the beginning. You should make clear all your expectations from the start to the potential spouse.

Is *deen* your most important criteria? If the intended person is not that religious, is that acceptable to you? What does marriage mean to you? What are your goals in life? Do you have educational or career requirements? What is your communication style? Do you want to have kids? What specific responsibilities do you believe a husband and wife should have? Is it okay for both the husband and the wife to work? Do you want to share your assets or would you prefer separate bank accounts? How much outside family involvement is acceptable

50. Abu Dawood

for both parties? How much alone time do you require? How do you handle change and the unexpected? How do you handle disagreements? Do you have any fears or reservations that need to be discussed? If either of the spouses has a physical or mental issue, this is the time to be honest about that. It is not fair to the intended to conceal this. In fact, if it comes out after the marriage and has an effect on the marriage, it is grounds for divorce.

The above-mentioned are simply guidelines. We like to plan and have our ideas, just as our parents may have for us, but marriage is also a form of ***rizq*** (provision) from Allah and it might come in a form we never expected. However, the more effort you put into researching and understanding, the higher the chances for success in your marriage. Ultimately, it is ***tawfiq*** (a gift of opportunity, aid, and blessing) from Allah, and even after all that, marriages could still fail. Nevertheless, the more effort you put into taking the right steps, just like studying for an exam, the more likely it will be for you to pass. In addition, since Allah is in control of all affairs, we should always make *du'aa* that He blesses us with a spouse that will be a comfort to our eyes and help us in *deen* and *dunya*.

SIGNS OF COMPATIBILITY IN MARRIAGE

SHARED VALUES

Sharing similar values and morals establishes a strong foundation. This foundation is further strengthened when your values both align with the *Qur'an* and *Sunnah*.

SHARED INTEREST

You don't have to like all the same things, but having some similar interests allows you to bond deeply and enjoy spending time together. These similarities can range from hobbies, intellectual interests, volunteer opportunities, and much more.

SIMILAR GOALS

Having similar goals creates a sense of shared purpose and direction in the relationship. These goals could include goals related to your deen, career, family, and personal growth.

POSITIVE FAMILY RELATIONS

Family is important, and in Islam our parents, siblings, and relatives have rights upon us. Therefore, it's important that you and your future spouse agree on continuing to have positive relationships based on respect with your respective families.

TRUST

As Muslims, we place all our *tawakkul* (trust) in Allah. However, it is also important to go into a marriage having trust that your spouse will fulfill your rights as you intend to fulfill theirs. Our inability to trust our spouse to fulfill our rights starts the marriage with instability.

OPENNESS TO COMPROMISE

If there is one theme that should be present throughout a marriage, it's the ability for both individuals to compromise. Be sure to look out to see if your future spouse is willing to compromise on certain things.

MARRIAGE ROLES

The term *"gender roles"* has a negative connotation in this day and age. Regardless of your stance on this topic, it's important that you and your future spouse come to a common ground when it comes to your roles in your marriage. This can include going over your expectations in situations when both spouses are working, how some of the responsibilities can be mutually shared, what are your roles in terms of taking care of elderly parents, and many such discussions. Although this topic can be uncomfortable for many, don't shy away from bringing it up.

PHYSICAL ATTRACTION

To say that physical attraction plays no role in spousal compatibility would be untrue. Being physically attracted to your future spouse is important in initiating the marriage and maintaining it over time. However, note that every human changes over time and our physical attraction is also impacted by our emotional connection and love for our spouse.

Get Your Parents Involved

It is important to involve your parents and family in the decision-making process and consider their future roles in your marriage. When Allah commands us to have *taqwa* and discusses the creation of man and woman, He immediately ends the ***ayah*** with the reminder of keeping family ties. Allah says,

"O mankind, fear your Lord, who created you from one soul and created from it its mate and dispersed from both of them many men and women. And fear Allah, through whom you ask one another, and the wombs. Indeed Allah is ever, over you, an Observer."[51]

In this *ayah*, *"and the wombs"* refers to family relations and family rights. [52] When entering a marriage, it is not just a union of two people but also the joining together of two families. Keeping this in mind, you must reflect on how compatible the family is and how much influence your family background and that of your intended will have upon your marriage. What roles will your parents and in-laws play in the decision-making process and in your married life? Will you live together with your spouse upon marriage or will you live with your family? Remember these are decisions that will affect your entire life and will directly impact your family relationships, so it is wise to be on the same page from the very beginning. Involving parents does not mean they should pressure or compel you to marry someone you are not happy with. You will be living with your spouse and your choice is what matters most. However, if you can, try to find someone that is pleasing to both you and your parents that will increase the chances of ***barakah*** (blessing) and diminish the chances of complications and difficulties you may have in the future.

---

51. Surah An-Nisaa' [4:1]
52. Tafsir At-Tabari

DID YOU KNOW?

Islam does not allow forced marriages. A woman cannot be forced to marry anyone she does not want to marry. The Prophet *sallAllahu 'alayhi wa sallam* told us,

"The maiden should not be given in marriage until her permission has been sought."

Buraydah ibn Al-Husayb [53] *radhiAllahu 'anhu* said,

"A girl came to the Prophet sallAllahu 'alayhi wa sallam and said: My father married me to his brother's son so that he might raise his own status thereby. The Prophet sallAllahu 'alayhi wa sallam gave her the choice, and she said: I approve of what my father did, but I wanted women to know that their fathers have no right to do that."

Character Matters

We should realize that marriage is not going to magically change one's character. So basically, what you see is what you get. Many people think they can change their potential spouse's character after marriage, and while that may be the case for a few, there are no guarantees. More likely than not, this will cause conflicts down the line, so it is important that you are pleased with the person's character at present and not with what they may become. The Prophet *sallAllahu 'alayhi wa sallam* advised us,

"If someone proposes marriage to you whose religion and character satisfies you, then you should accept it. If you do not do so, there will be trials on the earth and the spread of corruption." [54]

---

53. A companion of the Prophet *sallAllahu 'alayhi wa sallam*
54. At-Tirmidhi

DESIRABLE CHARACTERISTICS TO LOOK FOR IN A **SPOUSE**

PIOUS

A pious person is engrossed in seeking the pleasure of Allah, steers clear from the displeasure of Allah, and places Allah first in everything.

Marriage, like prayer, is an act of worship. Marrying someone who is pious ensures that you are both using your marriage as a means to draw closer to your Lord. This will also aid you both in fulfilling the rights you have upon each other.

RED FLAGS

Doesn't pray, disconnected from the *Qur'an*, doesn't put effort in following the *Sunnah*, has reservations about practicing Islam outwardly, etc. In some cases, a person may pray 5 times a day and fast, but have issues with honesty, trustworthiness, or being kind and gentle.

HONEST

An honest person is keen to always speak the truth and is focused on being sincere without pretense.

Honesty is one of the cornerstones of marriage. Failure to be honest with each other leads to a failed marriage.

RED FLAGS

Lying or omitting the truth, being known as a dishonest person, changing stories, etc.

FAIR

A fair person is objective and does not show favor based on bias, but makes decisions based on justice.

Selecting someone who is fair and just will give you the ease of knowing that they will deal with you with the utmost fairness in all matters.

RED FLAGS

Navigating from a place of bias, rushing into decisions without hearing all sides, etc.

KIND

A kind person is concerned for the feelings and wellbeing of others, both young and old.

Marriage is a beautiful but difficult task. You will be tested throughout your marriage with various opportunities to show each other kindness or be harsh with each other. A kind spouse will take your feelings and wellbeing into consideration before taking action on matters.

RED FLAGS

Harsh tone with others, unwelcoming body language with others, incites fear in family/others, etc.

CONSIDERATE

A considerate person gives careful thought when dealing with others and reflects on how their actions impact others.

The benefit of having a considerate spouse is that this individual will always contemplate on how their actions will impact you and your family together. They don't make decisions without consulting you and getting your perspective.

RED FLAGS

Narcissistic behavior, makes decisions without consultation, unwilling to understand how their actions impact others, etc.

WELL-MANNERED

A well-mannered person is polite and conducts oneself in the most appropriate way in various circumstances.

A well-mannered spouse is a mercy in all situations. This is an individual that is able to maintain courtesy and behave appropriately in whatever situation or environment they are in.

RED FLAGS

Hot tempered, behavior and situation misaligned, etc.

TRUSTWORTHY

A trustworthy person can follow through with their word or promise.

Trust is the most basic foundation of a marriage. Being in a marriage with an untrustworthy person comes with many anxieties and heartache. Imagine not having faith in anything your spouse says.

RED FLAGS

Lying, breaking promises, being two-faced with people, etc.

RELIABLE

A reliable person is dependable and shows up when needed.

If it's one thing that's for certain, you will need a partner that you can rely on, someone who will show up for you when you need them.

RED FLAGS

Disorganized, doesn't show up when needed, breaks promises, etc.

POSITIVE

A positive person is optimistic in nature and does not give in easily to negativity or hopelessness.

Negativity breeds negativity and the same can be said about positivity. Marriage and raising a family together will come with its highs and lows. It's important to have someone who is able to encourage you to remain positive and hopeful with the decree of Allah. This personality trait is one of the elements for success.

RED FLAGS

Hopeless, negative, constant complaining, unable to problem solve, questions *qadr (predestination)*, etc.

PATIENT

A patient person can remain calm in the face of adversity and maintain hope.

Patience is truly a virtue. Each individual is equipped with their respective flaws and struggles. A patient spouse will stand by you and work with you through your struggles and flaws.

RED FLAGS

Perfectionism, easily agitated, rushes to decision making, judgemental at a glance, etc.

CLEAN

A clean person prioritizes good hygiene and maintains a sanitary environment.

Cleanliness is half of our religion. Beautifying ourselves for our spouses is a highly regarded act of worship. A spouse who takes the time and energy to keep themselves and their environment clean brings joy to you and your household. The Prophet *sallAllahu 'alayhi wa sallam* said, *"Cleanliness is half of faith."* *

RED FLAGS

Disheveled, unkempt hygiene, unpleasant smells, dirty environment or living situation, etc.

STRONG

A strong person has the mental and physical strength to combat difficulty and hardship. Mental and physical strength are both deeply connected to introspection.

A spouse with mental and physical strength is able to go through the hurdles of life without needing constant aid. They will be able to look internally within themselves to find the strength to move through anything.

RED FLAGS

Crumbles at adversity, negative thinking patterns, unable to complete tasks, constant failure in many aspects of life, needy, etc.

* Sahih Muslim

GENEROUS

A generous person gives from their wealth and sacrifices their time and energy for others.

A generous spouse is one who will give themselves to you and your family. They understand generosity starts with our loved ones. They understand that this is more than just financial generosity, but rather sacrificing oneself for the betterment of their spouse and family.

RED FLAGS

Stingy, lacks empathy, doesn't volunteer or give back to the community, isn't involved with biological family, etc.

GENTLE

A gentle person is generally agreeable, kind, and lacks harshness.

Gentleness is not added to anything except it beautifies it. You will make many mistakes in your marriage and in your raising of a family. A gentle spouse is one that excludes harshness in their correcting of your mistakes and in their dealing with you and your family.

RED FLAGS

Harsh, quick to lash out, impatient, judgemental, critical, lacks soft speech, etc.

REASONABLE

A reasonable person approaches all matters with appropriate levels of caution and sensibility.

A reasonable spouse will not blow things out of proportion. They will use caution when making decisions that impact you and your family.

RED FLAGS

Irrational, lacks deep thought, lacks the ability to problem-solve, lacks foresight, etc.

INTELLIGENT

An intelligent person enjoys learning and utilizing their knowledge in productive ways.

An intelligent spouse will engage you in meaningful conversations and challenge you to be the best version of yourself. They are able to problem-solve and ponder deeply about life.

RED FLAGS

Lack of interest in self development, unable to make connections, lacks problem-solving capabilities, uninterested in seeking knowledge, etc.

MODEST

A modest person is humble about their abilities and talents.

Humility is a rare gem to come across. A humble spouse is one who is able to highlight your contributions without constantly reminding you about theirs. They are able to make up for what you lack at any given point without making a big deal about it. They conduct themselves appropriately with the opposite gender and remain in the Islamic attire that is required of them.

RED FLAGS

Boastful, arrogant, loud, inappropriate conduct with the opposite gender, fails to adhere to Islamic requirements for garments, etc.

FORGIVING

A forgiving person is intentional about letting go of resentment and vengeance against those who have wronged them.

A forgiving spouse is able to let go of your mistakes and makes it a point to not bring them up again. They do not seek revenge and are uninterested in remaining resentful toward you.

RED FLAGS

Holds on to grudges, brings up the past, focuses on your flaws and mistakes, etc.

LOVING

A loving person is affectionate and caring towards others.

Affection and care should remain in a marriage beyond the honeymoon stage. A loving spouse is one that affirms their love and devotion to you. They don't shy away from being vulnerable with you and are able to provide security.

RED FLAGS

Lacks vulnerability, stuck on cultural definitions of affection, fails to compliment, lacks emotional intelligence, etc.

EMPATHETIC

An empathetic person can comprehend and feel what others are going through.

An empathetic spouse is able to understand your circumstances and feel what you are going through. They make an effort to go through the hurdles and struggles with you. They are focused on teamwork and partnership.

RED FLAGS

Lacks emotional intelligence, judgemental, unable to make excuses for others, etc.

HAPPY

A happy person chooses to be cheerful in all situations.

Happiness is a choice. A spouse who chooses to be happy regardless of your situations is one that will find the light at the end of the tunnel. They wake up everyday and make the conscious effort to remain positive and upbeat.

RED FLAGS

Irritable, pessimistic, lacks humor, puts energy into remaining upset, unwilling to forgive or let go, etc.

MINDFUL

A mindful person remains conscious of their presence and its impact.

A mindful spouse is aware of how their actions and presence impacts everyone around them. They live in the moment and attempt to get the most out of their lives.

RED FLAGS

Heedless, oblivious, lacks self-awareness, lacks foresight, etc.

LEADER

A leader puts their goals into action and has the ability to inspire and motivate others.

Each spouse has their roles and each is a leader over an aspect of their marriage and family. A spouse with leadership skills is one with vision, goals, and motivation to be the best possible person they can be.

RED FLAGS

Lacks goals, lacks motivation, fails to show up, lacks accountability, selfish, etc.

ACTIVITY

Create your own "Make or Break" list.

Create a list of your top 10 "MUST HAVES" in your future spouse. These are the true non-negotiables that if the person doesn't have these present, it's a deal breaker. Some examples of *"must haves"* are: he must pray all his prayers in the *masjid*, she must be active in the community, he must have a good sense of humor, etc. Next, create a list of your top 10 "CAN'T STANDS" in your future spouse. We know that when people are interested in a potential spouse, they tend to forget about the red flags or may overlook their flaws. Can't stands are just as important as must haves because they will help you identify if this is the person you really want to marry and have a life with. Some examples of *"can't stands"* are: he is not courteous, she is loud when speaking, he is lazy, etc.

CHAPTER 6

TYING THE KNOT

The Pre-Requisites of Marriage

Before we get to the *nikaah*, there are some prerequisites that must be met. If one of these marriage prerequisites are not met, its absence will lead to the nullification of the action, and in this case, the marriage cannot and will not be valid. Here are the main prerequisites in marriage:

1. The bride and the groom both must be specified, and both must be known to each other. For example, a father who has three daughters cannot say, *"I'll marry you to one of my daughters."* He has to specify which one exactly. I marry you to such and such by name or by a description that could clearly mean no other.

2. Both the bride and the groom must approve and accept the marriage.

There can be no compulsion or force in marriage. As mentioned earlier, A girl came to the Prophet *sallAllahu 'alayhi wa sallam* and said,

"My father married me to his brother's son so that he might raise his own status, thereby. The Prophet sallAllahu 'alayhi wa sallam gave her the choice, and she said, 'I approve of what my father did, but I wanted women to know that their fathers have no right to do that.'" [55]

In another *hadith* the Prophet *sallAllahu 'alayhi wa sallam* said,

"The maiden should not be given in marriage until her permission has been sought." [56]

3 The approval of the ***wali*** (male guardian of the bride). If the *wali* does not accept the marriage, it cannot move forward. The Prophet *sallAllahu 'alayhi wa sallam* said,

"Any woman who gets married without the permission of her guardian, her marriage is invalid, her marriage is invalid, her marriage is invalid. But if the marriage is consummated then the mahr is hers because she has allowed him to be intimate with her. If they dispute, then the ruler [57] *is the guardian of the one who has no guardian."* [58]

4 There should be at least two sane Muslim witnesses to the marriage, and the marriage must be proclaimed publicly (i.e. no secret marriages). The Prophet *sallAllahu 'alayhi wa sallam* said,

"There is no marriage except with a guardian and two witnesses of good character." [59]

In another *hadith* the Prophet *sallAllahu 'alayhi wa sallam* said,

"Announce this marriage publicly, conduct it in the mosque, and strike the drums for it." [60]

5 There are no preventing or prohibited factors to the marriage. For example, marriages that are prohibited by blood relations, a bride and groom breastfed by the same mother, a person who has a mental illness, a Muslim man or Muslim woman marrying outside the religious restrictions that were mentioned earlier.

---

55. Ibn Majah
56. Sahih Al-Bukhari and Sahih Muslim
57. In a non-Muslim society an Imam of a *masjid* or a community or a Muslim scholar can fulfill this role.
58. At-Tirmidhi
59. Al-Bayhaqi
60. At-Tirmidhi

The Marriage Contract

After making sure both parties are compatible with one another and wanting to proceed, the only thing left is to have the ***nikaah*** (marriage). According to the majority of scholars, the marriage contract consists of:

1. Both parties fulfill the pre-conditions of marriage and do not have any preventing factors.

2. ***Ijaab*** (affirmation) [61] of the *wali* in which he or whoever takes his place says to the groom: *"**I marry you to** and he names the woman to be married."*

3. ***Qabool*** (acceptance) in which the groom or whoever takes his place says: ***"I accept."***

This is the correct way for the marriage to take place. The contract is between the *wali* and the groom. Nowadays, we see the facilitator [62] ask the bride instead of the *wali* and this is not the proper way. The bride has already accepted and agreed, so her representative, which is her *wali,* should speak on her behalf.

IMPORTANT TO KNOW

Even though the *nikaah* is a verbal contract, a marriage certificate is usually signed after the *nikaah* by the bride, the bridegroom as well as the witnesses and the person conducting the *nikaah*. The marriage certificate is the legal proof of the Islamic marriage and should be kept safe. In addition to nikaah, some countries and local laws may require the bride and bridegroom to record the marriage legally in their local jurisdiction. In some cases, you will need to obtain a marriage license from your local government office prior to the *nikaah*. This does not replace the *nikaah*. It merely records the marriage. Make sure to check your local laws prior to *nikaah*.

61. Refers to the offer, confirmation, or declaration from the *wali*.

62. The Imam or whoever is officiating the wedding.

The *Wali* (Male Guardian)

The *wali* must be Muslim, [63] male, sane, free, of age, just (upright, practicing, morally sound), and he must have proper decision-making capabilities. If a woman doesn't have a *wali*, she can go to the judge or trusted local imam to be her *wali*. If she has non-Muslim relatives, they are welcome to participate in the marriage celebration but in order for the marriage to be valid and Islamically correct, it must be done by a *wali* that is Muslim. [64]

The *Mahr* (Dowry)

The *mahr* (dowry) is one of the rights of the wife, which is hers to take lawfully. The *mahr* is usually monetary, but it could be anything agreed upon by the bride. Unfortunately, this contrasts with the widespread practice in some countries, where the wife is given no dowry or she and her family have to pay the dowry to the groom, which is not an Islamic practice. The *mahr* is not necessarily a condition for the *nikaah* to be correct, but it is something that is required. Allah says,

وَءَاتُوا۟ ٱلنِّسَآءَ صَدُقَـٰتِهِنَّ نِحْلَةً

"And give the women [upon marriage] their [bridal] gifts graciously." [65]

Ibn 'Abbas [66] *radhiAllahu 'anhu* said, *"This refers to the mahr (dowry)."* Most scholars commenting on this verse said: *"The man must definitely pay the dowry to the woman, and he should not resent it."* [67]

In another *ayah* Allah tells us,

وَإِنْ أَرَدتُّمُ ٱسْتِبْدَالَ زَوْجٍ مَّكَانَ زَوْجٍ وَءَاتَيْتُمْ إِحْدَىٰهُنَّ قِنطَارًا فَلَا تَأْخُذُوا۟ مِنْهُ شَيْـًٔا ۚ أَتَأْخُذُونَهُۥ بُهْتَـٰنًا وَإِثْمًا مُّبِينًا وَكَيْفَ تَأْخُذُونَهُۥ وَقَدْ أَفْضَىٰ بَعْضُكُمْ إِلَىٰ بَعْضٍ وَأَخَذْنَ مِنكُم مِّيثَـٰقًا غَلِيظًا

"But if you want to replace one wife with another and you have given one of them a great amount [in gifts], do not take [back] from it anything. Would you take it in injustice and manifest sin? And how could you take it while you have gone in unto each other and they have taken from you a solemn covenant?" [68]

This ***ayah*** clearly proves that a woman should be gifted *mahr*. As mentioned, if you want to divorce your wife and marry another, you should not take anything from what you have already given the first wife, even if it

63. A non-Muslim man cannot be a *wali* for a Muslim woman.
64. Please see the appendix for more details on "Who can be a *Wali*?"
65. Surah An-NIsaa' [4:4]
66. The cousin and companion of the Prophet *sallAllahu 'alayhi wa sallam* (d. 687). One of the greatest commentators (mufassir) of the *Qur'an*.
67. Tafsir Ibn Kathir
68. Surah An-Nisaa' [4:20-21]

was a huge amount of wealth. The *mahr* is given as a gift, and you have no right to take it back.

Anas ibn Malik [69] *radhiAllahu 'anhu* reported that 'AbdurRahman ibn 'Awf [70] *radhiAllahu 'anhu* came to the Messenger of Allah *sallAllahu 'alayhi wa sallam,* and there were traces of yellow (perfume) on him. The Messenger of Allah *sallAllahu 'alayhi wa sallam* asked him about it, and he told him that he had just married a woman of the *Ansar*. The Prophet *sallAllahu 'alayhi wa sallam* asked him, *"How much did you give her?"* He said: *"Gold equal to the weight of one date stone."* The Messenger of Allah *sallAllahu 'alayhi wa sallam* said: *"Have a walimah (wedding feast) even if only with one sheep."* [71]

What Should Be the Mahr?

The types of *mahr* varied during the time of the Prophet *sallAllahu 'alayhi wa sallam.* He *sallAllahu 'alayhi wa sallam* did not put a limit to the *mahr* or specify what form the *mahr* should be in. He *sallAllahu 'alayhi wa sallam* did encourage keeping the *mahr* simple and easy. He *sallAllahu 'alayhi wa sallam* said, *"The best of dowries is the simplest."* [72] Abu Salama [73] *radhiAllahu 'anhu* said, *"I asked 'Aisha about that and she said: 'The Messenger of Allah sallAllahu 'alayhi wa sallam got married (and married his daughters) for twelve Uqiyyah and a Nashsh'" which is five hundred dirhams."* [74]

'Umar ibn Al-Khattab *radhiAllahu 'anhu* said, *"'Do not go to extremes with regard to the dowries of women, for if that were a sign of honor and dignity in this world, or a sign of piety before Allah, the Mighty and Sublime, then the Prophet sallAllahu 'alayhi wa sallam would have done that before you. But he did not give any of his wives, and none of his daughters were given more than twelve Uqiyyah. A man may increase the dowry until he feels resentment against her and says: 'You cost me everything I own...'"* [75]

Sometimes the bride or the bride's family may stipulate a *mahr* that is an exorbitant amount beyond the groom's financial means. This should not be done. The *mahr* should be a reasonable amount based on the groom's financial capability.

---

69. Famous and last living companion of the Prophet *sallAllahu 'alayhi wa sallam* who was well-known for transmitting hadith. (d. 709AD)
70. One of the wealthiest companions of the Prophet *sallAllahu 'alayhi wa sallam* (d. 653AD) and he is one of the ten who was promised *Jannah.*
71. Sahih Al-Bukhari
72. Al-Hakim and Al-Bayhaqi
73. Famous companion of the Prophet *sallAllahu 'alayhi wa sallam* (d.625AD)
74. An-Nasaa'ee
75. An-Nasaa'ee

CAN THE WIFE **GIVE UP** HER MAHR?

It is permissible for the wife to give up her *mahr*. She can give all of it up, give a portion of it to her husband, or reduce it. It is her wealth and her right to do with it as she pleases.

Allah says, *"But if they give up willingly to you anything of it, then take it in satisfaction and ease."* [76]

Stipulating Conditions In Your Marriage Contract

It is allowed for the bride or groom to stipulate any conditions that do not go against the *Shari'ah* [77] of Islam or the foundation of a marriage contract.
The Prophet *sallAllahu 'alayhi wa sallam* said,

"...'What is the matter with some people who stipulate conditions that are not in the Book of Allah? Every condition that is not in the Book of Allah is invalid, even if there are one hundred conditions...'" [78]

Stipulations of conditions can only be done before the actual marriage (the *ijaab* and *qabool*). Once the marriage contract has been declared verbally or signed, you cannot come back and say you want to stipulate other conditions.

Examples of what can be stipulated; I would like to live in a mansion, or such and such for my *mahr,* or I don't want to move out of the city of my family. He or she can stipulate whatever they want as long as it is halal, and it is up to the husband to agree or not.

WHAT'S A **PRENUPTIAL AGREEMENT?**

A prenuptial agreement is "an agreement made between two people before marrying that establishes rights to property and support in the event of divorce or death." [79] It is not part of traditional Islamic marriage because both spouses already governed their marriage according to Islamic Law. In modern times, many people have moved away from the authentic teachings of Islam when it comes to marital rights, divorce, and even inheritance laws. It is for this reason that some scholars see a prenuptial agreement which defines the Islamic property rights of both spouses as permissible.

---

76. Surah An-Nisaa' [4:4]
77. A set of religious laws that have been legislated by Allah and revealed through His messenger *sallAllahu 'alayhi wa sallam* for our guidance.
78. Ibn Majah
79. Merriam-Webster

CHAPTER 5 & 6

REVIEW AND REFLECT QUESTIONS

1

Jennifer became Muslim two months ago and she is looking to get married, but no one else in her family is Muslim. Who should be appointed to safeguard her interests and why?

2

Every person has a list of characteristics that they would want in their spouse. List ten things that you are looking for in your ideal spouse. Explain why these characteristics are important for your spouse to have and how each one of these characteristics can contribute to a healthy marriage.

3

No one can be forced to marry anyone they don't like. At the same time, why is it important to make sure your parents agree and are accepting of the person you want to marry?

4

Asma and Hassan are getting married soon. Asma's father has asked Hassan for a huge amount of *mahr* in order to marry his daughter, which Hassan does not have. Hassan decides to get a second job to help cover the cost of the *mahr*. He is so tired from working two jobs and starts to have some resentment towards Asma's dad because he expects so much *mahr*. What should Hassan do?

CHAPTER 7

THE WALIMAH (WEDDING CELEBRATION)

A ***walimah*** (wedding celebration) is a celebration that is performed after the *nikaah.* The main purpose of a *walimah* is to publicize the marriage, and spread the news about it. Publicly announcing the marriage allows the community to be aware and know that the couple is married. The *walimah* is like *Eid* or an ***aqeeqah*** [80] and is a joyous occasion which we are encouraged to celebrate. The Prophet *sallAllahu 'alayhi wa sallam* said,

"Have a walimah (wedding feast) even if only with one sheep." [81]

Although there is no upper or lower limit to the cost of a *walimah*, it ideally should be within the budget of the couple and there should not be extreme waste. In over twenty *ayaat* in the *Qur'an,* Allah praises the middle path and reprimands those

80. The sacrifice of an animal on the occasion of the birth of a child.
81. Sahih Al-Bukhari

who spend in excess and who are wasteful. Allah says,

وَٱلَّذِينَ إِذَآ أَنفَقُوا۟ لَمْ يُسْرِفُوا۟ وَلَمْ يَقْتُرُوا۟ وَكَانَ بَيْنَ ذَٰلِكَ قَوَامًا

"And those who, when they spend, are neither extravagant nor stingy but hold a middle (path) between those (extremes)." [82]

In another ayah Allah says,

يَٰبَنِىٓ ءَادَمَ خُذُوا۟ زِينَتَكُمْ عِندَ كُلِّ مَسْجِدٍ وَكُلُوا۟ وَٱشْرَبُوا۟ وَلَا تُسْرِفُوٓا۟ ۚ إِنَّهُۥ لَا يُحِبُّ ٱلْمُسْرِفِينَ

"O children of Adam, take your adornment at every masjid, and eat and drink, but be not excessive. Indeed, He likes not those who commit excess." [83]

Sometimes people start to compete to see who can have the most lavish and extravagant *walimah*. From the *sunnah* of the Prophet *sallAllahu 'alayhi wa sallam* is that he had very simple weddings. Thus, we should keep in mind that the *walimah* should be done within your means to feed the guests and for the purpose of celebrating without breaking the bank and wastage. The Prophet *sallAllahu 'alayhi wa sallam* said,

"The easiest marriage is the best marriage." [84]

If you are invited to a *walimah*, it is highly encouraged that you accept the invitation and attend. The Prophet *sallAllahu 'alayhi wa sallam* said,

---

82. Surah Al-Furqan [25:67]
83. Surah Al-'Araf [7:31]
84. Abu Dawood
85. Sahih Al-Bukhari and Sahih Muslim

"The rights of a Muslim over his fellow Muslim are five: returning greetings, visiting the sick, attending funerals, accepting invitations, and saying Yarhamuk Allah (may Allah have mercy on you) when he sneezes." [85]

However, some scholars have said that a person has a right to refuse an invitation if they are aware that there will be *haram* aspects at the celebration such as alcohol, impermissible mixing, prohibited food and/or music. It is also disliked if only the rich are invited to a *walimah.* Abu Hurairah [86] *radhiAllahu 'anhu* narrated,

"The worst food is that of a wedding banquet to which only the rich are invited while the poor are not invited. And he who refuses an invitation (to a banquet) disobeys Allah and His Messenger." [87]

Du'aa For The Bride And Groom

It is from the *sunnah* to make *du'aa* for the bride and the groom. The Prophet *sallAllahu 'alayhi wa sallam* taught us these beautiful words,

بَارَكَ اللّٰهُ لَكَ وَبَارَكَ عَلَيْكَ وَجَمَعَ بَيْنَكُمَا فِي خَيْرٍ

"May Allah's blessing be for you and upon you and (may Allah) bring you both together in goodness." [88]

86. Famous companion of the Prophet *sallAllahu 'alayhi wa sallam* for narrating *hadith* (d. 678AD)
87. Sahih Al-Bukhari
88. Sahih Al-Bukhari and Sahih Muslim

WHEN CELEBRATING...

Start the marriage off in obedience to Allah and stay away from any acts that would be displeasing to Him. Allah says,

يَـٰٓأَيُّهَا ٱلَّذِينَ ءَامَنُوٓا۟ أَطِيعُوا۟ ٱللَّهَ وَأَطِيعُوا۟
ٱلرَّسُولَ وَأُو۟لِى ٱلْأَمْرِ مِنكُمْ
فَإِن تَنَـٰزَعْتُمْ فِى شَىْءٍ فَرُدُّوهُ إِلَى ٱللَّهِ
وَٱلرَّسُولِ إِن كُنتُمْ تُؤْمِنُونَ بِٱللَّهِ وَٱلْيَوْمِ
ٱلْـَٔاخِرِ ذَٰلِكَ خَيْرٌ وَأَحْسَنُ تَأْوِيلًا

"O you who have believed, obey Allah and obey the Messenger and those in authority among you. And if you disagree over anything, refer it to Allah and the Messenger, if you should believe in Allah and the Last Day. That is the best [way] and best in result." [89]

It is permissible to celebrate using the *daff* (a one sided drum), reciting poetry, singing *nasheed* (Islamic songs), playing games, and preparing a feast. Poetry and *nasheed* should encourage righteousness, uplift *imaan* (faith) and be free from musical instruments, immoral words and anything prohibited. The Prophet *sallAllahu 'alayhi wa sallam* said,

"Announce this marriage publicly, conduct it in the mosque, and strike the drums for it." [90]

Free mixing amongst the genders is not permitted, and presenting the bride and groom together goes against our Islamic values of modesty and etiquette. Abu Usayd Al-Ansari [91] *radhiAllahu 'anhu* narrated that he heard the Prophet *sallAllahu 'alayhi wa sallam* say to the women on his way out of the mosque when he saw men and women mixing together on their way home:

"'Give way (i.e., walk to the sides) as it is not appropriate for you to walk in the middle of the road.'

Thereafter, women would walk so close to the wall that their dresses would get caught on it." [92]

Dancing should be limited to women. [93] It should not be provocative or have

---

89. Sahih Al-Bukhari and Sahih Muslim
90. At-Tirmidhi
91. A companion of the Prophet *sallAllahu 'alayhi wa sallam* (d. 40AH)
92. Abu Dawood
93. Some scholars are of the opinion that dancing is not permissible by men as it resembles women, and some are of the opinion that there is no harm during celebrations as long as it is not imitating women or resembling the disbelievers. Further research can be done for your own benefit.

alluring movements which would reveal the woman's *'awrah* [94], it should not imitate the disbelievers, and it should not be done in front of men.

Dressing up should follow the Islamic guidelines, and adhere to being modest, loose, and covering the body properly. The Prophet *sallAllahu 'alayhi wa sallam* said,

"A man must not look at another man's 'awrah, nor must a woman look at another woman's 'awrah..."

Caution and discretion should be used if the wedding is being photographed or recorded. It is not permissible for a woman to share what is going on in the women's section with her husband or male relatives. The Prophet *sallAllahu 'alayhi wa sallam* said,

"No woman should look at another woman then describe her to her husband so that it is as if he can see her." [95]

---

94. *'Awrah:* The parts of the body which are considered private according to Islam and should be covered in the presence of others. Such as the chest to knee area for women in front of women and her entire body in front of men, excluding her face and hands. For men the *'awrah* is between the navel and knee. The meaning of *'awrah* may vary based on the context and based on differences in schools of thoughts of Islamic jurisprudence.

95. Sahih Al-Bukhari

DID YOU KNOW?

The responsibility of the walimah is all upon the husband. This is understood when the Prophet *sallAllahu 'alayhi wa sallam* said to 'Abd al-Rahmaan ibn *'Awf radhiAllahu 'anhu*,

"May Allah bless you. Give a walimah even if it is with just one sheep."

Scholars have said it is permissible for the *walimah* to be organized between the husband and wife as long as they are in agreement to that. Additionally, *walimah* expenses can also be shared if both families agree. However, if there is any disagreement at the end of the day, the responsibility is solely upon the husband.

UNIT 2

MARRIAGE: THE START OF A NEW JOURNEY TOGETHER

UNIT 2

IMPORTANT VOCABULARY

ADAB
Manners

AL-AHAD
The One, The Unique who is forever One and has never and will never have another alongside Him

AMANAH
Trust

'IDDAH
The prescribed period a woman must observe after the death of her husband or after a divorce, during which she may not marry another man

KHUL'A
Request for divorce or annulment of marriage initiated by the wife for compensation in exchange for the husband's consent

NAFL
Voluntary

SIWAK
A teeth-cleaning twig used at the time of the Prophet *sallAllahu 'alayhi wa sallam*

TALAAQ
Divorce

TABLE OF CONTENTS

UNIT 2 | MARRIAGE: A SACRED BOND

ESSENTIAL QUESTIONS

This unit is designed to help answer the following questions.

1. How does being mindful of Allah impact Islamic marriage?
2. Why are the roles of spouses different in a marriage?
3. How does self-centeredness affect a Muslim marriage?

CHAPTER 8

JUST MARRIED

You've selected your spouse, enjoyed the wedding ceremonies and events, and now it's time to start this new chapter of your life together. This relationship is unlike any other relationship due to the closeness, intimacy, and partnership found within it. This is also a relationship in which at its core is a form of worship, and with the permission of Allah will be a means of increasing the *ummah*. When approached from this perspective and navigated through the lens of the *Qur'an* and *Sunnah*, this relationship yields a beautiful love story and a means of entering *Jannah* together. Now let's get started on this journey, and what better way to start than through *du'aa* and *salah*?

Du'aa Of The Groom For The Bride

It is a *sunnah* for the groom to put his hand on the head of the bride and pray for her. The Prophet *sallAllahu 'alayhi wa sallam* said,

"If one of you marries a woman or buys a servant, he should take her by her forelock, mention Allah's name (saying bismillah) and pray for blessings by saying, "Oh Allah, I ask you for her good and the good of what you have dispositioned her toward and I seek refuge from her evil and the evil you have dispositioned her toward." [96]

Praying Together

It is *sunnah* for the groom to lead the bride and pray two *rakaats* together. As you start your new life as husband and wife, the best way to start your first real private moment together is by praying and seeking Allah's blessing in your marriage. The Prophet *sallAllahu 'alayhi wa sallam* said,

"When your wife enters upon you, pray two rak'ahs, then ask Allah, may He be exalted, for the good of what has entered upon you and seek refuge with Him from its evil, then go ahead and approach your wife." [97]

Keeping Intimate Details Private

Speaking about the private relations between you and your wife is absolutely forbidden. The Prophet *sallAllahu 'alayhi wa sallam* said,

"Among the worst type of people in the sight of Allah on the Day of Judgment is a man who enjoys his wife's intimate company, and she enjoys his intimate company, then one of them goes and discloses the secret of the other." [98]

---

96. Abu Dawood
97. Al-Musannaf of Abd Al-Razzaq Al-San'ani is an early *hadith* collection compiled by the eighth-century Yemeni scholar.
98. Sahih Muslim

To Honeymoon or Not To Honeymoon?

Some scholars are of the opinion that the honeymoon is an imitation of other cultures and ways of life. However, if the husband and wife simply intend to travel after marriage to spend time together, there should not be a problem. A few things should be kept in mind concerning the honeymoon:

The place of travel must be a permissible place, not involving any *haram* aspects. One should not be excessive or waste money.

One must not neglect personal obligations and religious duties. Many Muslims today follow the latest trends and ignore that as Muslims, every aspect of our life should be within the guidelines of the *Qur'an* and *Sunnah*. This includes how and where we go to celebrate our marriage. Allah says,

يَـٰٓأَيُّهَا ٱلَّذِينَ ءَامَنُوٓا۟ أَطِيعُوا۟ ٱللَّهَ وَأَطِيعُوا۟
ٱلرَّسُولَ وَأُو۟لِى ٱلْأَمْرِ مِنكُمْ فَإِن تَنَـٰزَعْتُمْ
فِى شَىْءٍ فَرُدُّوهُ إِلَى ٱللَّهِ وَٱلرَّسُولِ إِن كُنتُمْ
تُؤْمِنُونَ بِٱللَّهِ وَٱلْيَوْمِ ٱلْـَٔاخِرِ ذَٰلِكَ خَيْرٌ
وَأَحْسَنُ تَأْوِيلًا

"O you who have believed, obey Allah and obey the Messenger and those in authority among you. And if you disagree over anything, refer it to Allah and the Messenger, if you should believe in Allah and the Last Day. That is the best [way] and best in result." [99]

99. Surah An-Nisaa' [4:59]

DID YOU KNOW?

The Wife Maintains Her Last Name After Marriage

Contrary to various cultures where a woman was considered property of her husband with no right to her own name at marriage, nor rights to property, finances or inheritance, a Muslim woman maintains her last name and does not acquire her husband's last name. Maintaining her father's name ensures that her family's lineage is also preserved. This makes it possible for her offspring to know their maternal roots and maintain good family ties with them. Islam came to liberate women from these societal norms and elevate a woman’s status by giving her the right to maintain her own name and her identity. Islam also gives women the right to own property, inherit, vote, conduct businesses, etc.

Should A Wife Combine Her Bank Account With Her Husband's Account?

That is her choice. In Islam, any money that a Muslim woman earns from her job or businesses is her personal money. She is not obligated to share it with her husband or spend it on household expenditure. However, if she voluntarily wants to contribute, that is her choice.

ACTIVITY

Weddings should be celebrated and include halal fun. Imagine you are a wedding program planner who has to prepare a program for 6 hours. What would your program entail? What Islamic activities would you include? Thinking outside the box, create a fun and unique detailed hour by hour program to present to your class.

CHAPTER 9

MAINTAINING A HEALTHY RELATIONSHIP

To maintain a healthy relationship, the husband and wife must realize they are in a partnership sanctioned by Allah in order to better serve Him and benefit society at large. When you start your own new family, you must have a mindset that you are fulfilling an ***amanah*** (trust) from Allah. Both spouses must be willing to put in the work to make sure that the marriage is successful. The family is the building block of society, and if this building block is firm and sound, so will become society.

While working to maintain a relationship with your spouse and establishing your family, it is normal to fall short and make mistakes as the Prophet *sallAllahu 'alayhi wa sallam* said,

"All of the children of Adam make mistakes, and the best of those who make mistakes are those who repent." [100]

100. At-Tirmidhi

Striving For Taqwa[101]

When two people from different backgrounds and personalities live together, it is through *taqwa* that they can maintain good relationships and navigate various challenges of life. In the *Qur'an,* marriage is tied together with *taqwa* and being mindful of our family relationships. Allah says,

يَٰٓأَيُّهَا ٱلنَّاسُ ٱتَّقُوا۟ رَبَّكُمُ ٱلَّذِى خَلَقَكُم مِّن نَّفْسٍ وَٰحِدَةٍ وَخَلَقَ مِنْهَا زَوْجَهَا وَبَثَّ مِنْهُمَا رِجَالًا كَثِيرًا وَنِسَآءً وَٱتَّقُوا۟ ٱللَّهَ ٱلَّذِى تَسَآءَلُونَ بِهِۦ وَٱلْأَرْحَامَ إِنَّ ٱللَّهَ كَانَ عَلَيْكُمْ رَقِيبًا

"O mankind, fear your Lord, who created you from one soul and created from it its mate and dispersed from both of them many men and women. And fear Allah, through whom you ask one another, and the wombs (have taqwa of Allah in regard to family relations). Indeed Allah is ever, over you, an Observer." [102]

In another ayah Allah says,

يَٰٓأَيُّهَا ٱلَّذِينَ ءَامَنُوا۟ قُوٓا۟ أَنفُسَكُمْ وَأَهْلِيكُمْ نَارًا وَقُودُهَا ٱلنَّاسُ وَٱلْحِجَارَةُ عَلَيْهَا مَلَٰٓئِكَةٌ غِلَاظٌ شِدَادٌ لَّا يَعْصُونَ ٱللَّهَ مَآ أَمَرَهُمْ وَيَفْعَلُونَ مَا يُؤْمَرُونَ

"O you who have believed, protect yourselves and your families from a Fire whose fuel is people and stones, over which are [appointed] angels, harsh and severe; they do not disobey Allah in what He commands them but do what they are commanded." [103]

The scholars derive from this *ayah* that it is an obligation on every Muslim to teach their family members the basics of *Iman* and Islam along with Allah's commands and prohibitions. Realize that the *shayateen*, our forbidden desires, and society at large are trying to pull you towards the hellfire and you must be ever vigilant to avoid these traps and protect yourselves.

101. *Taqwa*: A sincere belief that Allah is always watching. Commonly translated as fear of Allah or God consciousness but it means more than that. It is an invisible barrier between you and the displeasure of Allah. This barrier is formed when you obey Allah and stay away from sin. *Taqwa* means to protect yourself from Allah's displeasure by obeying Him and staying away from His prohibitions.
102. Surah An-Nisaa' [4:1]
103. Surah At-Tahreem [66:6]

Being Kind & Patient

It is important for both spouses to practice being kind and patient towards one another. At times, you may come across a quality in your spouse that you dislike. However, no one should use a quality they dislike as an excuse to mistreat their spouse. At times like this, it is helpful to remember the many positive qualities that your spouse possesses.

Part of practicing patience and kindness is that when one spouse sees that the other is upset about something, they should not make things worse by adding fuel to the fire. Rather, they should maintain calmness in order to quiet the flame and make their spouse feel better. Allah says,

وَعَاشِرُوهُنَّ بِٱلْمَعْرُوفِ فَإِن كَرِهْتُمُوهُنَّ
فَعَسَىٰٓ أَن تَكْرَهُوا۟ شَيْـًٔا وَيَجْعَلَ ٱللَّهُ
فِيهِ خَيْرًا كَثِيرًا

"...And live with them in kindness. For if you dislike them - perhaps you dislike a thing and Allah makes therein much good." [104]

The Prophet *sallAllahu 'alayhi wa sallam* said,

"A man should not make his wife angry if he sees in her something that he dislikes, because if he dislikes one of her characteristics, he will like another" and "No believing man should hate a believing woman, if he dislikes one of her characteristics, he will like another." [105]

Being Understanding

An understanding individual is able to conduct themselves in a calm and appropriate manner in various situations. There will be times when you notice a fault in your spouse, want to complain about something they said or did, or even want to scold them. At these times, keep in mind the importance and value of being an understanding spouse.

---

104. Surah An-Nisaa' [4:19]
105. Sahih Muslim

Empathy is a part of understanding. When you practice empathy, that means you try to understand the situation of another person. If you notice your spouse has a fault or is falling short in an area, remember that there are times when you also make mistakes and fall short. During those times, do you appreciate it when others put you down or make efforts to lift you up?

Similarly, instead of pointing out flaws, complaining, or scolding your spouse, try to share words of encouragement and engage in actions that will lift them up. Perhaps you can even pick up the slack in the area that you see them faltering.

Anas Ibn Malik *radhiAllahu 'anhu* narrated,

"While the Prophet sallAllahu 'alayhi wa sallam was in the house of one of his wives, one of the mothers of the believers sent a meal in a dish. The wife at whose house the Prophet sallAllahu 'alayhi wa sallam was, struck the hand of the servant, causing the dish to fall and break. The Prophet sallAllahu 'alayhi wa sallam gathered the broken pieces of the dish and then started collecting on them the food which had been in the dish and said, "Your mother (my wife) felt jealous." Then he detained the servant till a (sound) dish was brought from the wife at whose house he was. He gave the sound dish to the wife whose dish had been broken and kept the broken one at the house where it had been broken." [106] [107]

Notice how the Prophet *sallAllahu 'alayhi wa sallam* did not admonish her or shame her for her actions, but rather calmed the situation, explained her behavior, and came up with a solution. Also, observe the humbleness of the Prophet *sallAllahu 'alayhi wa sallam*. Instead of asking her or the servant to clean it up, he did it himself!

Abu Darda said to his wife Umm Darda *radhiAllahu 'anhum,*

"If I become angry, then try to please me. If you become angry, then I will try to please you. Were we not to act this way, how quickly would we be separated!" [108]

---

106. Sahih Al-Bukhari
107. The narrator *radhiAllahu 'anhu* was using a high form of adab (manners) and did not mention the name of the wife in order to cover her faults.
108. Ibn Hibban

Having Good Communication

Good communication is a vital part of all relationships and is an essential part of a healthy marriage. All marriages experience ups and downs, but practicing healthy communication skills can make it easier to deal with conflict and build a stronger and healthier marriage. Part of healthy communication skills in a marriage is being able to advise each other in a gentle and wise manner. Only through this are you able to hold each other accountable and bring your hearts closer to Allah.

'Umar *radhiAllahu 'anhu* asked the Prophet *sallAllahu 'alayhi wa sallam,*

"'O Messenger of Allah, what kind of wealth should we acquire?' He said: 'Let one of you acquire a thankful heart, a tongue that remembers Allah and a believing wife who will help him with regard to the Hereafter.'" [109]

How we speak with each other is critical in marriage. Allah has asked us,

"And speak kindly to people" [110]

The Prophet *sallAllahu 'alayhi wa sallam* was asked once to tell of something that will guarantee paradise. He *sallAllahu 'alayhi wa sallam responded,*

"Speak kind words, offer peace, and feed the hungry." [111]

109. Ibn Majah
110. Surah Al-Baqarah [2:83] This *ayah* can be recited in two different ways. One recitation gives the meaning of good speech in general and in another recitation, it gives the meaning of beauty, i.e., the way you talk to others and the speech you use with others should be one of beauty that has gentleness and benefit.
111. Ibn Hibban

4 WAYS TO EFFECTIVELY **COMMUNICATE** WITH YOUR SPOUSE

1 ADDRESSING EACH OTHER

While living together, sometimes spouses tend to take each other for granted and may address or call one another in a harsh or sarcastic manner. Over time, this can build up feelings of resentment. It is very important to choose nice words and the best of names for your spouse. The Prophet *sallAllahu 'alayhi wa sallam* exhibited his love for his wife in the way he addressed her. It is known that he used to lovingly call his wife Aisha *radhiAllahu 'anha*, Ya A'ish.

2 REQUESTING FROM EACH OTHER

Always ask and request from each other in a respectful manner. A husband should not request something from his wife in a belittling manner as if she is a servant. In the same way, a wife should not ask her husband for something by making him feel bad about himself. Asking each other in the best loving manner accompanying it with a *du'aa* and showing appreciation makes any mundane or difficult task easy.

3 CONVERSING WITH EACH OTHER

As important as it is to converse with each other in a nice manner, it is also important to converse at an appropriate time. Conversing when one spouse is busy, stressed for time, or tired is not wise and may cause a harsh or rude response. Being respectful of each other's time along with speaking in a gentle, loving tone increases understanding, love, and respect for each other.

4 HANDLING DIFFERENCE OF OPINIONS & ARGUMENTS

Being wise in handling differences of opinions and preventing arguments is critical in a marriage. Sometimes if we feel hurt or are angry, we may not address these situations in the best manner. Remember, exploding in anger and arguing is a sign of a hypocrite. The Prophet *sallAllahu 'alayhi wa sallam* said, *"I guarantee a house in the outskirts of Paradise to the one who leaves arguing even if he is right."*

In situations where you feel you have been wronged or mistakes have been made, point out the mistake in a calm and kind manner. The goal is to correct the mistake and not to hurt feelings.

If a spouse is angry, don't escalate the situation by responding in a similar manner. Being patient during this time will not only deescalate the situation, but you will be rewarded for your patience by Allah. Responding to anger with anger can lead to other problems and statements which will be later regretted.

Remember not to respond to harshness with harshness, but rather with kindness, and you will eventually win your spouse over. If you are patient and seek your reward from Allah, He will replace your hardships with ease. Some scholars say that the *ayah* stating *"and we amended his wife for him"* [112] in reference to Prophet Zakariyyah *'alayhis salaam* was a response to his patience with her harshness, and Allah made her soft and kind to him and provided him with a child at an old age.

---

112. Surah Al-Anbiyaa [21:90]

Learning Together

What better way to maintain a healthy relationship than by learning about your *deen* together? Instead of watching a movie, going out, or doing some other mundane activity, make sure you make time for each other to seek knowledge and help each other in good deeds. The Prophet *sallAllahu 'alayhi wa sallam* said,

"Seeking knowledge is obligatory on every Muslim." [113]

In another *hadith*, the Prophet *sallAllahu 'alayhi wa sallam* said,

"May Allah have mercy upon a man who wakes up at night and prays, and awakens his wife. If she refuses, he sprinkles water on her face. May Allah have mercy upon a woman who wakes up at night and prays, and awakens her husband. If he refuses, she sprinkles water on his face." [114]

Being Respectful To Each Other

Sometimes, we find that we have an amazing character with friends and strangers, yet when we are in the privacy of our home, we do not have the best of manners towards our families. This is the opposite of the *sunnah*. If we are kind, good mannered and patient with strangers, we should be even more so with our own spouses. The Prophet *sallAllahu 'alayhi wa sallam* said, *"I have been sent to perfect good character."* [115]

In another *hadith* he *sallAllahu 'alayhi wa sallam* said, *"The most complete of the believers in faith, is the one with the best character among them. And the best of you are those who are best to your women."* [116]

113. Ibn Majah
114. Ibn Majah
115. Al-Muwatta
116. At-Tirmidhi

Giving Each Other The Benefit Of The Doubt

Giving your spouse the benefit of the doubt not only helps you avoid harmful negative feelings, but it also promotes positivity and patience in your marriage. Failure to make excuses for your spouse can also cause your spouse to jump into a defensive mode rather than hearing you out. An easy way to practice the act of making excuses for each other can be found in the idea of being curious rather than furious. This can be done by seeking to understand why certain things happen or why your spouse behaves in a certain way rather than reacting with anger or another strong emotion. It leads you to think deeply and make excuses for your spouse rather than making judgements and assumptions. Allah says,

يَٰٓأَيُّهَا ٱلَّذِينَ ءَامَنُوا۟ ٱجْتَنِبُوا۟ كَثِيرًا مِّنَ ٱلظَّنِّ إِنَّ بَعْضَ ٱلظَّنِّ إِثْمٌ ۖ وَلَا تَجَسَّسُوا۟ وَلَا يَغْتَب بَّعْضُكُم بَعْضًا

"O you who have believed, avoid much [negative] assumption. Indeed, some assumption is sin. And do not spy or backbite each other." [117]

There are many statements from the companions that support finding excuses for one another. Ja'far ibn Muhammad [118] *rahimahullaah* said,

"If you hear something from your brother that you reject, make an excuse for him up to seventy excuses. If you cannot do it, then say: Perhaps he has an excuse I do not know." [119]

To have a mutually respectful relationship, you and your spouse should have good intentions towards one another and know that each of you wants goodness for the other. You must navigate from a place of love and compassion, especially during difficult times. Remind yourself that your spouse only wants good for you, and their shortcomings are truly unintentional. The best way to accomplish this is to constantly renew your intentions. Just like all acts of worship, remind yourself of your goal, the pleasure of Allah. In the process of having good thoughts about your spouse and renewing your intentions, don't forget to make *du'aa* for yourself, your spouse, and your marriage. The Prophet *sallAllahu 'alayhi wa sallam* said,

"No Muslim servant supplicates for his brother behind his back but that the angel says: And for you the same." [120]

---

117. Surah Al-Hujuraat [49:12]
118. The great, great grandson of the Prophet *sallAllahu 'alayhi wa sallam* (d.148AH)
119. Al-Bayhaqi
120. Sahih Muslim

Looking Nice For Each Other

The desire and drive to look your best when stepping out of your house has been a century long pressure from society. From the way we style our dresses to the color coordination of our sneakers, we are constantly pushed to care more about how well put together we are. What is not emphasized or prioritized is how we look for our spouses. The Prophet *sallAllahu 'alayhi wa sallam* said,

"The best women (spouses) are those that if you look at them, they are pleasing to you." [121]

Ibn Abbas [122] *radhiAllahu 'anhu* used to say, *"Verily, I love to beautify myself for my wife, just as I love for her to beautify herself for me, due to Allah saying: "They have similar rights to those over them."* [123]

Thanking Each Other

Practicing gratitude has many benefits that range from increased happiness to developing a sense of purpose. Did you know that showcasing gratitude with your spouse also aids your marriage? Spouses that practice gratitude with each other have a more positive feeling towards each other and they tend to have a stronger bond and connection. The Prophet *sallAllahu 'alayhi wa sallam* said, *"Whoever does not thank the people is not thankful to Allah."* [124]

And in another *hadith* he *sallAllahu 'alayhi wa sallam* said, *"If someone does something good for you, compensate them in like and if you are unable to, make du'aa for them."* [125]

Gratefulness and appreciation will lead to love and consideration for each other, whereas constant complaints and ungratefulness will lead to hard feelings and resentment.

---

121. Al-Bayhaqi
122. Famous companion of the Prophet *sallAllahu 'alayhi wa sallam*, He is considered the greatest commentator of the *Qur'an* (d.687AD)
123. An-Nasaa'ee
124. Ahmad
125. Abu Dawood

Showing Love For Each Other

The Prophet *sallAllahu 'alayhi wa sallam* was always keen to enter his house in the best of manners. He would use the ***siwak*** (a teeth-cleaning twig) so that he would have an even more pleasant scent for his family. Shurayh [126] *radhiAllahu 'anhu* reported,

I asked 'Aisha, saying, "What was the first thing the Prophet, sallAllahu 'alayhi wa sallam, did when he entered his house?" 'Aisha said, "Use the toothstick." [127]

When he exited the house, he would show love by kissing his wife. He always tried to make his family happy. When 'Aisha *radhiAllahu 'anha* would try to give him a drink, he would refuse to take it. She would insist, and he would swear he would not drink from it until she drank. After she drank, he would drink from the same spot to show his love for her and make her feel special and happy. 'Aisha *radhiAllahu 'anha* said,

"... The Messenger of Allah sallAllahu 'alayhi wa sallam would call me to eat with him while I was menstruating. He would take a piece of bone on which some bits of meat were left and insist that I take it first, so I would nibble a little from it, then put it down. Then he would take it and nibble from it, and he would put his mouth where mine had been on the bone. Then he would call for a drink and insist that I take it first before he drank from it. So I would take it and drink from it, then put it down, then he would take it and drink from it, putting his mouth where mine had been on the cup."" [128]

Doing Things for The Sake of Allah

Another way to achieve good character in marriage is to do things for the sake of Allah and not expect anything in return (i.e., don't do something to receive something in return). This way, you will never be disappointed and your spouse will learn to do the same. If you do a good deed or help your spouse, don't keep reminding them about it. Allah says,

يَـٰٓأَيُّهَا ٱلَّذِينَ ءَامَنُوا۟ لَا تُبْطِلُوا۟ صَدَقَـٰتِكُم بِٱلْمَنِّ وَٱلْأَذَىٰ

"O believers! Do not waste your charity with reminders of your generosity or hurtful words..." [129]

---

126. Shurayh Al-Harathi: He was from the *Tabi'een* (A generation of Muslims who came after the companions of the Prophet *sallAllahu 'alayhi wa sallam* and never met the Prophet *sallAllahu 'alayhi wa sallam*) A scholar of *Fiqh*, a warrior and a leader. (d. 78AH)
127. Sahih Muslim
128. An-Nasaa'ee
129. Surah Al-Baqarah [2:264]

Fulfilling Each Other's Rights

Both spouses must work together to fulfill each other's rights in the hopes to be rewarded, protected from haram, and keep each other chaste. The Prophet *sallAllahu 'alayhi wa sallam* said,

"O 'Abdullah! Have I not been informed that you fast all day and stand in prayer all night?" I said, "Yes, O Allah's Messenger sallAllahu 'alayhi wa sallam!" He said, "Do not do that! Observe the fast sometimes and also leave them (the fast) at other times; stand up for the prayer at night and also sleep at night. Your body has a right over you, your eyes have a right over you ***and your wife has a right over you."*** [130]

SOME WAYS TO BUILD A STRONG RELATIONSHIP

- Spend quality time together.
- Communicate clearly with each other.
- Listen to each other.
- Pay attention to your spouse's wants and needs.
- Be understanding.
- Pray and learn together.
- Be kind and generous to each other.
- Thank your spouse regularly.
- Help each other with tasks and chores.
- Build and maintain trust with each other.
- Treat each other like you would like to be treated.

130. Sahih Al-Bukhari

CHAPTER 9

REVIEW AND REFLECT QUESTIONS

1

Khalid's childhood friend is getting married and has informed him that he will be having a mixed wedding in which there will be singing, dancing, and several group activities and games."*This is a once in a lifetime occasion, man. I'm going to make sure that we celebrate until 3am!*" says Khalid's friend. Khalid doesn't want to attend the wedding because of the *haram* aspects that will occur. Write a letter to his best friend explaining kindly and with wisdom why he won't be able to attend his friend's wedding.

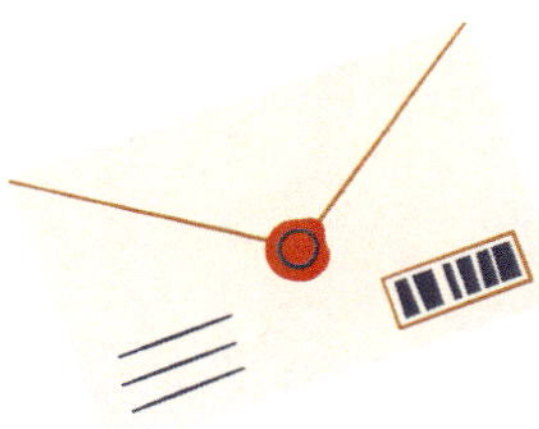

2

Having good manners is an extremely important part of every relationship. Manners don't just miraculously become perfect once you get married. We all have different areas related to our conduct in which we need to improve, and it's good to work towards improvement well before getting married. What is something you know you need to work on, and what steps will you take to improve yourself in this area? Some examples are: quick to be angered, having an unforgiving character, having lack of patience, having a cursing nature, etc.

3

It is inevitable to have arguments in a marriage. No relationship can escape that. However, just like we have a Fire Escape plan, we should have our own *"Argument Escape"* plan. Do some research on how to deal with confrontations and arguments. Then, create an infographic on how you would like you and your future spouse to resolve situations. Support your infographic with two hadith.

4

The Prophet *sallAllahu 'alayhi wa sallam* said, ***"Whoever does not thank people has not thanked Allah."*** [131] List some ways that you can show appreciation to your spouse.

131. Abu Dawood

CHAPTER 10

MUTUAL RIGHTS & RESPONSIBILITIES IN MARRIAGE

Allah has created everyone unique, beautiful, and different in their own way. There are no two people who are exactly alike. Allah has made these differences amongst us so that we may learn from each other, help each other grow, and most importantly learn to appreciate these differences. This especially holds true in our marriages. You will never get a better introduction to the opposite gender than you do in marriage. It is through this union that you will come to see the major differences between the two genders. Allah has created us both differently and thus has different expectations of us. Through His infinite Mercy and Wisdom, He has adjusted our roles and responsibilities to match our inherent biological, psychological, and physical strengths. Only through this understanding and appreciation of our differences are we able to truly fulfill our rights, roles, and responsibilities in our marriages. Allah says,

يَـٰٓأَيُّهَا ٱلنَّاسُ إِنَّا خَلَقْنَـٰكُم مِّن ذَكَرٍ وَأُنثَىٰ وَجَعَلْنَـٰكُمْ شُعُوبًا وَقَبَآئِلَ لِتَعَارَفُوٓا۟ إِنَّ أَكْرَمَكُمْ عِندَ ٱللَّهِ أَتْقَىٰكُمْ إِنَّ ٱللَّهَ عَلِيمٌ خَبِيرٌ

"O mankind, indeed We have created you from male and female and made you peoples and tribes that you may know one another. Indeed, the most noble of you in the sight of Allah is the most righteous of you. Indeed, Allah is All-Knowing, All-Aware." [132]

In another *ayah* Allah says,

وَلَيْسَ ٱلذَّكَرُ كَٱلْأُنثَىٰ

"... and the male is not like the female..." [133]

'Aisha radhiAllahu 'anha *narrated that the Prophet* sallAllahu 'alayhi wa sallam *said, "Verily, women are the twin halves of men."* [134]

Our differences are there to complement each other and help build patience in our understanding and interactions with our spouses. When we understand the greater purpose of our differences, it becomes easier for us to fulfill our roles, rights, and obligations in the marriage.

Both men and women have defined roles, rights, and responsibilities as spouses in marriage. True marital happiness is highly dependent on fulfilling those rights. When the wife protects the rights of her husband and the husband protects the rights of his wife, we can see the love and mercy grow between them. This is because they are obeying Allah in their responsibilities towards each other. Therefore, it is very important for us to learn about our rights and the rights of our spouse before entering into a marriage. Allah says,

وَلَهُنَّ مِثْلُ ٱلَّذِى عَلَيْهِنَّ بِٱلْمَعْرُوفِ وَلِلرِّجَالِ عَلَيْهِنَّ دَرَجَةٌ وَٱللَّهُ عَزِيزٌ حَكِيمٌ

"And they (women) have rights (over their husbands) similar (to those of their husbands) over them, but men have a degree (of responsibility) over them." [135]

When going into a marriage, focusing on our duties and being aware of each other's rights will help create a well-balanced relationship. This, in turn, will lead to a family life full of love, peace, empathy, and stability.

---

132. Surah Al-Hujuraat [49:13]
133. Surah Ale-Imran [3:36]
134. Abu Dawood
135. Surah Al-Baqarah [2:228]

RIGHTS OF THE HUSBAND

1 TO LEAD THE FAMILY

Allah in His Wisdom has given certain qualities to men and certain qualities to women. Allah has created men generally to have strength, courage, independence, and leadership qualities. The husband's responsibility in marriage is to take care of his family by providing financial security as well as protection from any harm. The right to be the head of the household has been given to him by Allah. Allah says,

ٱلرِّجَالُ قَوَّٰمُونَ عَلَى ٱلنِّسَآءِ بِمَا فَضَّلَ ٱللَّهُ بَعْضَهُمْ عَلَىٰ بَعْضٍ وَبِمَآ أَنفَقُوا۟ مِنْ أَمْوَٰلِهِمْ ۚ فَٱلصَّٰلِحَٰتُ قَٰنِتَٰتٌ حَٰفِظَٰتٌ لِّلْغَيْبِ بِمَا حَفِظَ ٱللَّهُ

"Men are in charge of women by [right of] what Allah has given one over the other and what they spend [for maintenance] from their wealth. So righteous women are devoutly obedient, guarding in [the husband's] absence what Allah would have them guard." [136]

This verse clearly gives the leadership of the family to the man. If we look at teams, companies, organizations, states or countries, there is usually one main leader and this makes for more efficient development, direction, and growth. Having leadership does not mean there shouldn't be consultation or consideration with the spouse. It means that the man has the responsibility to ensure that all matters pertaining to his spouse and family are taken care of appropriately, done according to the *Qur'an* and the *Sunnah,* and that fairness and justice are observed. After all, with great responsibility comes great accountability. The Prophet *sallAllahu 'alayhi wa sallam* said,

"Every one of you is a shepherd and is responsible for his flock. The leader of people is a guardian and is responsible for his subjects. A man is the guardian of his family and he is responsible for them. A woman is the guardian of her husband's home and his children and she is responsible for them. The servant of a man is a guardian of the property of his master and he is responsible for it. No doubt, every one of you is a shepherd and is responsible for his flock." [137]

---

136. Surah An-Nisaa' [4:34]
137. Sahih Al-Bukhari and Sahih Muslim

The man should view the right being in charge through a lens of guidance and caretaking, and not one of dictatorship or oppression. When a woman knows her husband will take her needs into consideration and she gives this right to him out of respect and obedience to Allah, it usually leads to marital harmony and a successful partnership and foundation.

2 TO BE RESPECTED

Allah has given the husband the huge responsibility of protecting, providing, and leading his family. For him to fulfill this enormous task, his wife and children should be keen to respect him and listen to his advice. It is impossible to protect and lead people who are unwilling to trust your leadership and listen to your guidance. *"Behind every strong man is a stronger woman."* Although it is a cliché, there is so much truth to this saying. A husband can only remain strong and fulfill his duties if he has a supportive wife who understands his daunting task and rather than competing with him, aids him in fulfilling it. The Prophet *sallAllahu 'alayhi wa sallam* stressed the status of the husband in front of his wife in the following *hadith*,

"If I were to order anyone to prostrate himself before another, I would have ordered the wife to prostrate herself before her husband." [138]

The Prophet *sallAllahu 'alayhi wa sallam* has told us about the great reward that a woman has for doing her part in the family by listening to her husband. He *sallAllahu 'alayhi wa sallam* said,

"If a woman prays her five prayers, fasts her month of Ramadan, guards her chastity, and obeys her husband, she will enter Paradise from any gate she wishes." [139]

However, this obedience is conditional and cannot be against what Allah or His Prophet *sallAllahu 'alayhi wa sallam* has asked us to do or to stay away from. As The Prophet *sallAllahu 'alayhi wa sallam* told us,

"There is no obedience to any created being if it involves disobedience towards the Creator." [140]

138. At-Tirmidhi
139. Ibn Hibban
140. Ahmad

3 TO SEEK CONSULTATION

Consultation and cooperation in a marriage shows that you not only trust your spouse, but that you also value and respect their opinion. Consulting each other enhances your bond and avoids the possibility of resentment and blame. In a healthy and loving marriage, both spouses must practice mutual consultation in all important matters. Similar to the rules of making ***shuraa*** (the process of decision-making by consultation), after consultation, the final decision lies with the responsible party. In a marriage and family, the responsibility and accountability fall on the husband. Therefore, the wife should make it a point to consult her husband and trust his final decision. This does not mean that the husband should not consult or consider the opinion and viewpoint of his wife. It means that he is accountable in front of Allah for any consequences that arise from his decisions. The Prophet *sallAllahu 'alayhi wa sallam* said,

"It is not permissible for a woman to fast [141] *when her husband is present except with his permission, or to allow anyone in his house without his permission."* [142]

It is the duty of the husband to ensure that no one with ill intent has access to his family and that he is aware of his family's whereabouts. If there is an understanding between the husband and wife, it is not necessary for the wife to seek permission before inviting someone into the home or going somewhere.

The Prophet *sallAllahu 'alayhi wa sallam* said, *"... You have rights over your women and your women have rights over you. As for your right upon them, that they should protect your honor and not allow someone in your home that you disapprove of..."* [143]

By fulfilling these rights guided by Allah and His messenger *sallAllahu 'alayhi wa sallam,* a woman should know that she is not deficient in any way. Rather, she is fulfilling her responsibility and part in marriage. By doing this, first and foremost she is pleasing Allah, as the the Prophet *sallAllahu 'alayhi wa sallam* said,

"Any woman dies while her husband is pleased with her, she will enter Jannah." [144]

Secondly, she is contributing to building a strong family, community and a society.

---

141. This is with regards to any voluntary fasts. No permission is needed for mandatory fasts like *Ramadan*.
142. Sahih Al-Bukhari
143. At-Tirmidhi
144. At-Tirmidhi

ADDITIONAL POINTS TO REMEMBER

With the huge responsibility of raising upright, caring, and productive individuals as well as maintaining the smooth running of the household on the women's shoulders, there are additional roles and responsibilities which when practiced mutually, create a caring and loving family striving to please Allah.

A wife should protect her husband's wealth by spending it wisely and not being wasteful, but see it as a trust to be managed in the best interest of her family.

Both the husband and wife should protect the family's honor, raise the children to respect both parents, teach them good character, and teach them the foundations of Islam.

One of the greatest evils in Islam is backbiting. Therefore, in a marital relationship, the wife should not disparage or turn her children against her husband nor should she teach them to disrespect him. He is their father and her husband, and she should be the best example to her children in how they treat their father by not involving them in marital conflict. Just as she expects her husband to do for her, a wife should refrain from talking negatively to anyone about her husband when there is an argument or any marital discord.

Both the husband and wife should protect the confidentiality of their marriage. This is one of the sacred trusts and must be honored at all times. She should not allow friends, family, or acquaintances to negatively influence her against her husband. Allah says, *"...So righteous women are devoutly obedient, guarding in [the husband's] absence what Allah would have them guard..."* [145]

She should work towards fulfilling her responsibility of maintaining the home through its various household chores). [146] The husband should also help around the house. Aisha *radhiAllahu 'anha* was asked, what did the Prophet *sallAllahu 'alayhi wa sallam* used to do in his house? She *radhiAllahu 'anha* said, 'He *sallAllahu 'alayhi wa sallam* was in the service of his family..." [147]

If the husband is unable to maintain the expenses of the family and the wife needs to work, there should be a more equitable share in the duties of the household. If she needs help in maintaining her home and she is able to hire help or the husband can afford to hire help for her, then there is nothing wrong in doing so.

145. Surah An-Nisaa' [4:34]
146. There is a difference of opinion on this matter. Please refer to the appendix for details on this issue.
147. Sahih Al-Bukhari

RIGHTS OF THE WIFE

Allah, the All-Just and All-Wise in His Justice and Wisdom has given rights to women as He has given rights to men. Allah says,

وَلَهُنَّ مِثْلُ ٱلَّذِى عَلَيْهِنَّ بِٱلْمَعْرُوفِ وَلِلرِّجَالِ
عَلَيْهِنَّ دَرَجَةٌ ۗ وَٱللَّهُ عَزِيزٌ حَكِيمٌ

"... And they (women) have rights (over their husbands) similar (to those of their husbands) over them, but men have a degree (of responsibility) over them." [148]

The Prophet *sallAllahu 'alayhi wa sallam* advised the men by telling them,

"I advise you to treat women kindly, for the woman was created from a rib, and the most crooked part of the rib is its uppermost part. If you try to straighten it, you will break it; and if you leave it, it will remain crooked. So, treat women kindly." [149]

In another *hadith*, he *sallAllahu 'alayhi wa sallam* said, *"The best of you are the best to their families, and I am the best to my family..." Let us look at how the husband should fulfill his wife's rights, how he should provide and properly take care of her, and how he can be considered the best to his family."* [150]

1 TO PROVIDE GUIDANCE

One of the greatest responsibilities a husband has towards his wife is to help guide her upon the *Qur'an* and the *Sunnah*. If a man does not care how his family is with Allah, then he is not truly fulfilling his duty towards them. Allah says,

وَأْمُرْ أَهْلَكَ بِٱلصَّلَوٰةِ وَٱصْطَبِرْ عَلَيْهَا لَا
نَسْـَٔلُكَ رِزْقًا نَّحْنُ نَرْزُقُكَ وَٱلْعَـٰقِبَةُ لِلتَّقْوَىٰ

"And enjoin prayer upon your family [and people] and be steadfast therein. We ask you not for provision; We provide for you, and the [best] outcome is for [those of] righteousness." [151]

---

148. Surah Al-Baqarah [2:228]
149. Sahih Muslim
150. At-Tirmidhi
151. Surah Taha [20:132]

When guiding one's wife, the husband must be wise in the way he speaks and he should never resort to any oppressive form of communication. Whenever he needs to advise or would like something from his wife, he owes her the respect to speak to her with dignity and with the best of manners. Allah says,

ٱدْعُ إِلَىٰ سَبِيلِ رَبِّكَ بِٱلْحِكْمَةِ وَٱلْمَوْعِظَةِ
ٱلْحَسَنَةِ

"Call to the Way of your Lord with wisdom and kind advice..." [152]

2 TO PROVIDE FINANCIAL SECURITY

A husband should provide food, clothing, and financial assistance within his means and capabilities. Allah tells us,

لِيُنفِقْ ذُو سَعَةٍ مِّن سَعَتِهِۦ وَمَن قُدِرَ عَلَيْهِ
رِزْقُهُۥ فَلْيُنفِقْ مِمَّآ ءَاتَىٰهُ ٱللَّهُ لَا يُكَلِّفُ ٱللَّهُ نَفْسًا
إِلَّا مَآ ءَاتَىٰهَا سَيَجْعَلُ ٱللَّهُ بَعْدَ عُسْرٍ يُسْرًا

"Let a man of wealth spend from his wealth, and he whose provision is restricted - let him spend from what Allah has given him. Allah does not charge a soul except [according to] what He has given it. Allah will bring about, after hardship, ease." [153]

The Prophet *sallAllahu 'alayhi wa sallam* said,

" ...And their right over you is that you should treat them kindly with regard to their clothing and food... " [154]

152. Surah An-Nahl [16:125]
153. Surah At-Talaaq [65:7]
154. At-Tirmidhi

3 TO PROVIDE A HOME

It is the responsibility of the husband to provide a decent and safe home for his wife according to his means. If he is wealthy, it should be in line with what he can afford, and if he is struggling financially, he should provide according to what he is capable of. Ibn Qudaamah [155] *rahimahullaah* said, *"She (the wife) is entitled to accommodation because Allah says,*

أَسْكِنُوهُنَّ

"Lodge them ..." [156]

If it is obligatory to provide lodgings (housing) for a divorced wife, then it is even more appropriate that lodgings should be provided for one who is still married." [157]

155. Famous Scholar of *fiqh* (d. 620AH)
156. At-Talaaq [65:6]
157. Al-Mughni

4 TO BE TREATED FAIRLY & KINDLY

The Prophet *sallAllahu 'alayhi wa sallam* was the epitome of fairness, kindness, and understanding to his wives. Even though he had the weight of the *ummah* upon his shoulders and his responsibilities were more than any great leader recorded in history, he would still come home and help out his wives, joke with them, and be present for them. Allah says,

وَعَاشِرُوهُنَّ بِٱلْمَعْرُوفِ

"And live with them in kindness." [158]

The Prophet *sallAllahu 'alayhi wa sallam* said, *"I advise you to treat your women kindly..."* [159]

He *sallAllahu 'alayhi wa sallam* further advised the men,

"Fear Allah regarding women. Verily, you have taken them as a trust from Allah, and intimacy has been made lawful by the word of Allah." [160]

158. Surah An-Nisaa' [4:19]
159. Sahih Al-Bukhari and Sahih Muslim
160. Sahih Muslim

DID YOU KNOW?

It is not acceptable to mock and make fun of your spouse. We aren't referring to the lighthearted teasing that spouses may have with each other. We are talking about the mockery that causes your spouse to become angry, undermines their self-worth, and makes them feel inadequate. When you mock or make fun, you are conveying to your spouse that you don't really value them. Allah tells us,

يَـٰٓأَيُّهَا ٱلَّذِينَ ءَامَنُوا۟ لَا يَسْخَرْ قَوْمٌ مِّن قَوْمٍ عَسَىٰٓ
أَن يَكُونُوا۟ خَيْرًا مِّنْهُمْ وَلَا نِسَآءٌ مِّن نِّسَآءٍ عَسَىٰٓ
أَن يَكُنَّ خَيْرًا مِّنْهُنَّ وَلَا تَلْمِزُوٓا۟ أَنفُسَكُمْ وَلَا
تَنَابَزُوا۟ بِٱلْأَلْقَـٰبِ بِئْسَ ٱلِٱسْمُ ٱلْفُسُوقُ بَعْدَ
ٱلْإِيمَـٰنِ وَمَن لَّمْ يَتُبْ فَأُو۟لَـٰٓئِكَ هُمُ ٱلظَّـٰلِمُونَ

"O you who have believed, let not a people ridicule [another] people; perhaps they may be better than them; nor let women ridicule [other] women; perhaps they may be better than them. And do not insult one another and do not call each other by [offensive] nicknames. Wretched is the name of disobedience after [one's] faith. And whoever does not repent - then it is those who are the wrongdoers." [161]

161. Surah Al-Hujuraat [49:11]

CHAPTER 11

WHEN ALL ELSE FAILS

There are many reasons why marriages experience difficulties: poor communication, different parenting styles, financial situations, etc. Every marriage will go through its fair share of arguments and disputes. However, if these arguments and disputes become more than normal and continue to happen without any resolution, it is recommended to seek counsel or involve intermediaries to try to get to the root of the issues and make peace. Some people think that pursuing counseling means your relationship is *'failing,'* but that couldn't be further from the truth. It is actually a positive step towards learning how to solve issues with more compassion and it can help rebuild a marriage. Allah says,

وَإِنْ خِفْتُمْ شِقَاقَ بَيْنِهِمَا فَٱبْعَثُوا۟ حَكَمًا مِّنْ
أَهْلِهِۦ وَحَكَمًا مِّنْ أَهْلِهَآ إِن يُرِيدَآ إِصْلَـٰحًا
يُوَفِّقِ ٱللَّهُ بَيْنَهُمَآ ۗ إِنَّ ٱللَّهَ كَانَ عَلِيمًا خَبِيرًا

"And if you fear dissension between the two, send an arbitrator from his people and an arbitrator from her people. If they both desire reconciliation, Allah will cause it between them. Indeed, Allah is ever Knowing and Acquainted [with all things]." [162]

And in another *ayah* Allah tells us,

وَٱلصُّلۡحُ خَيۡرٞ

"Making peace (between each other) is better." [163]

The Prophet *sallAllahu 'alayhi wa sallam* said, *"A believing man should not leave a believing woman, if he dislikes something in her, there is something in her he is pleased with."* [164]

In another *hadith* he *sallAllahu 'alayhi wa sallam* told us, *"Should I not tell you of something that is even better than (extra) fasting, prayers, and charity?" The companions said: "Of course, oh messenger of Allah!" He said:* ***Making peace between two parties****. For verily, fighting between each other is the razor and I don't say it shaves (destroys) the hair but it destroys the deen."*

Islam always encourages reconciliation in marriage, especially if there are children involved. The Prophet *sallAllahu 'alayhi wa sallam* said to Barira [165] *radhiAllahu 'anha* the wife of Mugheeth [166] *radhiAllahu 'anhu*, *"Won't you stay with him? He is the father of your child."* [167]

Ways To End The Marriage

Even with the best intentions, sometimes there are irreconcilable differences in a marriage. For this reason, Allah in His infinite Wisdom and Mercy has legislated ***talaaq*** (divorce). A relationship that has constant fighting and no progression is unhealthy and can cause damage to the household and be particularly impactful if children are involved. Sometimes one of the parents may be acting in a manner that is detrimental to the children, and it is better for them not to witness that behavior. In this case, it is not appropriate to force a couple to stay together.

Unlike other cultures and religions, Islam allows the end of marriage. For example, in Catholicism, *talaaq* is illegal and in fact can cause someone to be excommunicated from their church. In Hinduism, the wife, no matter what the circumstances, has no right to ask for separation. However, Allah knows

162. Surah An-Nisaa' [4:35]
163. Surah An-Nisaa' [4:128]
164. Sahih Muslim
165. Female companion of the Prophet *sallAllahu 'alayhi wa sallam*
166. A companion of the Prophet *sallAllahu 'alayhi wa sallam*
167. Sahih Al-Bukhari

that people may change, and as spouses change, conflict may arise. Allah has made *talaaq* a viable solution to solve problems. Let's learn a little more about what a couple's options are when things seem to be going downhill in their marriage. In Islam, there are two ways to end a marriage:

1. ***TALAAQ*** (Divorce)

2. ***KHUL'A*** (Divorce or annulment of marriage initiated by the wife)

1 WHAT IS TALAAQ?

Talaaq literally means to depart or break away. It is the only legitimate avenue to end a marriage. Although *talaaq* is not something encouraged or desired, if it is done with the proper Islamic ***adab*** (manners) [168] , it can actually bring about much benefit such as peace between the spouses, family, and society. It also can open the doors to a fresh start.

Islamically, *talaaq* is the dissolution or annulment of the marriage contract with specific language. The specific language is clearly stating there is a divorce such as: *"I divorce you"* or using language that is understood to mean divorce, with the intention of divorce such as: *"You are no longer my wife?"*

The following conditions must be fulfilled for the *talaaq* to be valid:

A. It must be pronounced by the husband.

B. He must be sane, of age, and under no coercion.

If the husband has lost his faculties (physically or chemically induced) or he has become so angry that he does not know what he is doing (temporary insanity), the *talaaq* is not valid. There is also a waiting period of about three months for the divorce to become final. If the spouses decide to make up during this waiting period, then they can continue the marriage. This divorce is considered one divorce. *Talaaq* can happen up to three times, on three separate occasions. If after the third time the spouses decide not to get back together after the waiting period, then the divorce is considered irrevocable and is final. In this case, the spouses must part ways and cannot remarry each other unless the woman marries someone else and is divorced from that person.

Talaaq is legislated by Allah in the *Qur'an,* the *Sunnah* of the Prophet *sallAllahu 'alayhi wa sallam*, and *Ijmaa'*.

168. Ending according to the *Shari'ah* and in an amicable manner without being abusive, revengeful, or unjust.

DID YOU KNOW?

In the studies of fiqh there are five Islamic rulings on *talaaq*:

1. **WAJIB** (Obligatory): It is obligatory if either spouse is abstaining from fulfilling each other's rights or if either of them is doing something clearly haram. This also applies if the wife disregards the leadership and advice of her husband.

2. **MUSTAHAB** (Preferred): It is preferred to divorce if he has no desire for her whatsoever and she is not helping him to be chaste.

3. **MUBAH** (Permitted): It is permissible if there is a reason for it, for example, the spouses no longer like each other.

4. **MAKROOH** (Disliked): It is disliked if he divorces for no reason.

5. **MUHARAM** (Forbidden): It becomes haram if he divorces her for no reason and it causes harm to her. It is also haram if he divorces at the times it is prohibited to divorce her. [169]

---

169. During her menses cycle or during a period when they were intimate.

Talaaq In The *Qur'an*

Allah tells us in the *Qur'an*,

"Divorce is twice. Then, either keep [her] in an acceptable manner or release [her] with good treatment. And it is not lawful for you to take anything of what you have given them unless both fear that they will not be able to keep [within] the limits of Allah . But if you fear that they will not keep [within] the limits of Allah , then there is no blame upon either of them concerning that by which she ransoms herself. These are the limits of Allah , so do not transgress them. And whoever transgresses the limits of Allah - it is those who are the wrongdoers." [170]

In another *ayah* Allah says,

وَإِن طَلَّقْتُمُوهُنَّ مِن قَبْلِ أَن تَمَسُّوهُنَّ وَقَدْ
فَرَضْتُمْ لَهُنَّ فَرِيضَةً فَنِصْفُ مَا فَرَضْتُمْ إِلَّآ أَن
يَعْفُونَ أَوْ يَعْفُوَا۟ ٱلَّذِى بِيَدِهِۦ عُقْدَةُ ٱلنِّكَاحِ
وَأَن تَعْفُوٓا۟ أَقْرَبُ لِلتَّقْوَىٰ وَلَا تَنسَوُا۟ ٱلْفَضْلَ
بَيْنَكُمْ إِنَّ ٱللَّهَ بِمَا تَعْمَلُونَ بَصِيرٌ

"And if you divorce them before consummating the marriage but after deciding on a dowry, pay half of the dowry, unless the wife graciously waives it or the husband graciously pays in full. Graciousness is closer to righteousness. And do not forget the kindness amongst yourselves. Surely Allah is All-Seeing of what you do." [171]

Allah reminds us in this *ayah* to not forget the kindness and goodness that the spouses had while married. Divorce is not a walk in the park. It takes a toll on the couple, their families, their finances, and their overall wellbeing. Many walk away with feelings of bitterness, regret, and immense sadness. If you are going through a divorce, always remember that you once shared a life with this person in the most intimate manner and cared for this person very deeply. If the marriage didn't work out, always do your best to leave on good terms.

---

170. Surah Al-Baqarah [2:229]
171. Surah Al-Baqarah [2:237]

Talaaq In The Sunnah

Ibn 'Umar *radhiAllahu 'anhu* reported,

"I divorced my wife during the lifetime of Allah's Messenger sallAllahu 'alayhi wa sallam when she was in the state of menses. 'Umar radhiAllahu 'anhu made a mention of it to Allah's Messenger sallAllahu 'alayhi wa sallam, whereupon he said: Command him to take her back and leave her (in that state) until she is purified. Then (let her) enter the period of second menses, and when she is purified, then divorce her (finally) before having relations with her, or retain her (finally). That is the 'Iddah (the prescribed period) which Allah commanded (to be kept in view) while divorcing the women..." [172]

It is reported by Ali [173] *radhiAllahu 'anhu,*

"No one who divorces according to the sunnah will be regretful." [174]

Talaaq Is Agreed Upon By Ijmaa'

(Consensus of Scholars)

Ijmaa', as mentioned before, is a unanimous agreement on a particular matter among the scholars of Islam after the death of the Prophet *sallAllahu 'alayhi wa sallam* during any era. The scholars of the Muslim *ummah* have unanimously agreed that *talaaq* is a part of Islam and is something permissible.

---

172. Sahih Muslim
173. Famous companion of the Prophet *sallAllahu 'alayhi wa sallam* and 4th *Khalifah* (leader) of the Muslims.
174. Al-Mughni by Ibn Qudamah

DID YOU KNOW?

Talaaq is a serious matter! It's not something to take lightly or even joke about! The Prophet *sallAllahu 'alayhi wa sallam* said,

"There are three matters in which it is not permissible to joke: marriage, divorce, and freeing of slaves." [175]

Thus, if someone is joking with their friend and says, *"I divorced my wife,"* it counts!

And if someone is joking with his spouse, *"I divorce you,"* it actually counts as one divorce!

IRREVOCABLE DIVORCE

Divorce is a serious matter. According to the scholars of Islamic Jurisprudence, irrevocable divorce [176] is when the husband and wife are not allowed to marry each other after three divorces occur. All scholars agree that the *sunnah* of divorce is to occur on three

175. Sahih Muslim

176. The husband and wife are not allowed to remarry each other unless the wife marries someone else sincerely and genuinely gets divorced from that person then she is allowed to remarry her first husband. She must be sincere in her intentions of marriage and have relations with her new husband. It is absolutely forbidden to have a marriage of convenience in order for her to go back to her previous husband and the curse of Allah is upon someone who does such an act.

separate occasions during the marriage, along with its 3 separate waiting periods.

What happens when a husband divorces his wife by saying it 3 times on one occasion?

If a husband divorces his wife by saying three times, *"I divorce you"* on one occasion, it is considered *haram* and an innovation. According to the majority of scholars such a divorce counts as 3 divorces and the couple is divorced irrevocably. However, there are a minority of the scholars who consider a divorce pronounced 3 times on one occasion as one divorce. They also agree that such divorce is not according to the *sunnah* of the Prophet *sallAllahu 'alayhi wa sallam* and such divorce is considered *haram* and an innovation. This shows the gravity of a divorce and that it should not be taken lightly or abused. If a couple is considering divorce after exhausting all other means, it is best to consult with an Imam or someone who is knowledgeable in Islamic Jurisprudence to help them during this process.

How does divorce occur on 3 separate occasions according to the Sunnah?

#1

When a husband pronounces the divorce one time on one occasion, then the couple has the opportunity to make up during the waiting period [177] and return to marital life.

If they make up after the waiting period is over, then they must get remarried (with a *nikaah* (marriage contract), *mahr*, etc.) to each other in order to continue marital relations. This is considered the 1st divorce.

#2

If it happens again (the second divorce) the same ruling as the first applies.

#3

If the third pronouncement of divorce occurs, they are not allowed to marry each other. It is too late, and they have burned through the chances Allah has given to them.

This becomes the irrevocable divorce and the only way they could ever get remarried is if the wife happens to marry another person and genuinely gets divorced which of course is a very difficult and highly unlikely outcome. This, again, is to emphasize the serious consequences of divorce and to prevent divorce on trivial things.

177. A divorce waiting period in Islam usually consists of the wife's 3 menstrual cycles (3 months). If the wife is pregnant then it is considered until the child is born. It is best to get an Imam or someone well versed in Islamic jurisprudence to get involved during the divorce proceedings.

2 KHUL'A

At times, a woman may truly desire to end the marriage but the husband refuses to divorce her for whatever reason. In this case, a woman can turn to the option of ***khul'a,*** which is the request for divorce or annulment of marriage initiated by the wife. *Khul'a* literally means taking off or removing something. If a *khul'a* is granted, the marriage ends faster than a divorce (*talaaq*). The woman must return her *mahr* to her husband in order to divorce herself from him. If the husband refuses to consent to the *khul'a,* a judge/imam has the right to dissolve the marriage.

Allah mentions *khul'a* in the *Qur'an,*

وَلَا يَحِلُّ لَكُمْ أَن تَأْخُذُوا۟ مِمَّآ
ءَاتَيْتُمُوهُنَّ شَيْـًٔا إِلَّآ أَن يَخَافَآ أَلَّا يُقِيمَا
حُدُودَ ٱللَّهِ ۖ فَإِنْ خِفْتُمْ أَلَّا يُقِيمَا حُدُودَ
ٱللَّهِ فَلَا جُنَاحَ عَلَيْهِمَا فِيمَا ٱفْتَدَتْ بِهِۦ ۗ
تِلْكَ حُدُودُ ٱللَّهِ فَلَا تَعْتَدُوهَا وَمَن يَتَعَدَّ
حُدُودَ ٱللَّهِ فَأُو۟لَـٰٓئِكَ هُمُ ٱلظَّـٰلِمُونَ

"And it is not lawful for you (men) to take back (from your wives) any of your mahr (dowry given by the husband to his wife at the time of marriage) which you have given them, except when both parties fear that they would be unable to keep the limits ordained by Allah (e.g. to deal with each other on a fair basis). Then if you fear that they would not be able to keep the limits ordained by Allah, then there is no sin on either of them if she gives back (the mahr or a part of it for her khul'a annulment)." [178]

Khul'a is mentioned in the story of the wife of Thabit ibn Qays ibn Shammaas [179] *radhiAllahu 'anhu* who came to the Prophet *sallAllahu 'alayhi wa sallam* and said,

"O Messenger of Allah, I do not find any fault with Thabit ibn Qays in his character or his religious commitment, but I do not want to commit any act of kufr after becoming a Muslim." The Prophet sallAllahu 'alayhi wa sallam said to her, "Will you give back his garden?" Because he had given her a garden as her mahr. She said, "Yes." The Prophet sallAllahu 'alayhi wa sallam said to Thabit: "Take back your garden, and divorce her."

178. Surah Al-Baqarah [2:229]
179. Famous companion of the Prophet *sallAllahu 'alayhi wa sallam*, served as one of his orators and scribes.

REASONS FOR KHUL'A

It is not fair for a woman to be forced to stay with her husband if she does not want to do so. In the studies of *fiqh*, here are some Islamic rulings on *khul'a*:

1. MUBAH (Permitted):

If the spouse dislikes her husband's character, his physical looks, deficiency in his religion, or if she fears to be sinful if she is not able to fulfill her husband's rights, she is permitted to ask for *khul'a*. This also applies if he is mistreating or causing harm to her.

2. MAKROOH (Disliked):

It is disliked if the wife asks for *khul'a* for no particular reason.

3. MUHARAM (Forbidden):

Some scholars say it is *haram* if she asks for *khul'a* for no reason. This is to discourage taking the sacred bond of marriage lightly. The Prophet *sallAllahu 'alayhi wa sallam* said, "*If a woman asks her husband for a divorce, for no reason, then the smell of Paradise is forbidden for her.*" [180]

WISDOM OF DIVORCE IN ISLAM

Allah in His wisdom has given three chances to divorce. Mistakes in marriage may happen from either the husband or the wife or both. If it is from the husband and he divorces, he may realize his mistakes and appreciate her more. Likewise, if it was from the wife and he divorces her twice, she can realize this is serious and try to rectify the situation. If it comes to the third time, it is too late for both, and they will realize they cannot be together anymore unless the woman marries again and by chance divorces.

Another wisdom from the Islamic divorce method is that the woman stays in her marital home during her waiting period. This can facilitate the chances of both spouses realizing their mistakes and making peace with one another.

180. At-Tirmidhi

CHAPTER 11

REVIEW AND REFLECT QUESTIONS

1

You are sitting in a gathering of friends, and the conversation takes a turn towards a married friend venting out frustration and annoyance about their spouse. You notice that this friend is slowly beginning to get comfortable in opening up frustrations, minor differences, and pet peeves about their spouse. You are torn between whether you should encourage your friend to continue talking and sharing their frustrations or if you should try to steer the conversation in a different direction. What would you do and why?

2

Fatima has seen her mom always complaining about her dad. Since childhood, she has formed a negative impression of her dad and is scared of him even though he has always been kind and caring towards her. Today, Fatima, is upset at her husband because he had to go into work this weekend while she had made plans for them to go out of town with the children. In her anger, she wants to vent to her children and make them think badly of him so they can show him some attitude. *"Don't you see that your dad doesn't care about any of us? He only cares about his work,"* she tells her kids. What mistake is Fatima making in this scenario? What would you advise her to do differently?

3

A friend of yours is looking to get married and will soon be meeting with a potential spouse. As your friend prepares for their meeting, they approach you for advice. *"I anticipate that when meeting with this person, they will ask me about my views and expectations on the rights and responsibilities of a husband and wife in a marriage. I want to answer this question from an Islamically-correct viewpoint, but I am not confident about my knowledge in this area."* How would

you advise your friend to approach this question? In your answer, make sure to elaborate on each point that you learned about in Chapters 10 and 11.

4

Your friend has recently been having some conflicts in their marriage. They have found themselves arguing with their spouse about the way they want to raise their kids, the lack of time being spent together as a family, and disagreements about the way their money is being spent. Your friend feels that the marriage has come to a standstill and it is time to part ways with their spouse. However, their spouse has expressed that they want to work on the marriage by seeking marriage counseling. How would you advise your friend in this situation while keeping in mind that Islamically, divorce is allowed but reconciliation is encouraged? Create a list of steps that you would advise your friend to follow before making a final decision about their marriage.

APPENDIX

Who Can Be A Wali?

The *wali* is the male guardian of the woman. He is entrusted to safeguard the interests of the woman. We cannot choose anyone to be our *wali*. In general, the father is the *wali* or anyone who the father appoints. In his absence or under certain situations an Imam of a community or a Muslim judge, governor or leader can take his place. The *wali* must fulfill the conditions previously mentioned, and if one of those conditions is not met, you can go to the *wali* next in line. Additionally, if the *wali* is not fulfilling his obligation, he can be replaced by a Muslim leader or Imam. The *wali* must be in the order mentioned below: If there are no relatives available from the paternal side or if they do not fit the Islamic legal requirements, the woman can turn to the Judge in Muslim countries or the local Imam in non-Muslim societies. If she has a maternal relative that she would like to represent her as a *wali,* the Judge or the Imam can appoint them to be her *wali* as long as he fulfills the Islamic requirements.

1. **FATHER**
2. **ANYONE THE FATHER APPOINTS**
3. **THE GRANDFATHER FROM THE FATHER'S SIDE** (includes the great grandfather and great great grandfather), and however far up they may ascend.
4. **THE SON** (includes the grandson, great-grandson, and great-great-grandson, and however far down they may descend.)
5. **THE BROTHER FROM THE SAME FATHER AND MOTHER**
6. **THE BROTHER FROM THE SAME FATHER**
7. **THE NEPHEW** (from her brother
8. **HER UNCLE FROM THE FATHER'S SIDE AND THEN HIS MALE CHILDREN**
9. **THEN WHOEVER IS CLOSEST FROM THE FATHER'S SIDE OF THE FAMILY**

---

181. If living in a non-Muslim majority country.
182. If in a predominately Muslim society.
183. Scholars have put together a list of who can be a *wali*. Men from the paternal side are listed since Scholars felt that they would be more inclined in protecting the interest of the bride since they share the same family name.
184. Please refer to section "THE *WALI* (MALE GUARDIAN)" for more details.
185. It is extremely important that if you need to choose an Imam as your wali, you must choose based on his righteousness, adhering to the *Qur'an* and the Sunnah and avoid any Imams that would be questionable or not look out for your benefit. The purpose of the wali is for him to protect and safeguard the woman.

HOW TO PRAY SALAAT-UL-ISTIKHAARAH?

Salaat-ul-istikhaarah is performed exactly like any *nafl* (voluntary) prayers. In the last *rak'ah* before the salaam (in the sitting position), you need to make a *du'aa* seeking Allah's advice on the matter at hand. This is done by saying the *du'aa* of *istikhaarah* as told to us by the Prophet *sallAllahu 'alayhi wa sallam*. After making the *du'aa*, you can say the salaam. You can now make the decision based on what you feel is right (considering you have done your due diligence by researching the matter and consulting with experts or scholars). If the decision is good for you, everything will proceed smoothly. However, if the decision is not good for you, there may be hurdles and obstacles in your path, and this could be an indication that this may not be the right decision. However, it could be that you proceed through the obstacles and it works out. The main purpose of *istikhaarah* is to consult Allah in your endeavors and accept whatever the outcome may be. Allah knows the future, therefore, He knows what is best for everyone.

اللَّهُمَّ إِنِّي أَسْتَخِيرُكَ بِعِلْمِكَ، وَأَسْتَقْدِرُكَ بِقُدْرَتِكَ، وَأَسْأَلُكَ مِنْ فَضْلِكَ الْعَظِيمِ، فَإِنَّكَ تَقْدِرُ
وَلَا أَقْدِرُ، وَتَعْلَمُ، وَلَا أَعْلَمُ، وَأَنْتَ عَلَّامُ الْغُيُوبِ، اللَّهُمَّ إِنْ كُنْتَ تَعْلَمُ أَنَّ هَذَا الْأَمْرَ خَيْرٌ
لِي فِي دِينِي وَمَعَاشِي وَعَاقِبَةِ أَمْرِي عَاجِلِهِ وَآجِلِهِ فَاقْدُرْهُ لِي وَيَسِّرْهُ لِي ثُمَّ بَارِكْ لِي
فِيهِ، وَإِنْ كُنْتَ تَعْلَمُ أَنَّ هَذَا الْأَمْرَ شَرٌّ لِي فِي دِينِي وَمَعَاشِي وَعَاقِبَةِ أَمْرِي عَاجِلِهِ وَآجِلِهِ
فَاصْرِفْهُ عَنِّي وَاصْرِفْنِي عَنْهُ وَاقْدُرْ لِيَ الْخَيْرَ حَيْثُ كَانَ ثُمَّ أَرْضِنِي بِهِ

"O Allah, I seek Your guidance [in making a choice] by virtue of Your knowledge, and I seek ability by virtue of Your power, and I ask You of Your great bounty. You have power, I have none. And You know, I know not. You are the Knower of hidden things. O Allah, if in Your knowledge, this matter (then it should be mentioned by name) is good for me both in this world and in the Hereafter (Or: in my religion, my livelihood and my affairs), then ordain it for me, make it easy for me, and bless it for me. And if in Your knowledge it is bad for me and for my religion, my livelihood and my affairs (or: for me both in this world and the next), then turn me away from it, [and turn it away from me], and ordain for me the good wherever it may be and make me pleased with it." [186]

---

186. Sahih Al-Bukhari

Is It Mandatory For Women To Do Household Chores?

There is a difference of opinion amongst the scholars on this issue. Some scholars say that it is encouraged, but not obligatory, for women to do household chores. Others say it is obligatory because of how the Prophet *sallAllahu 'alayhi wa sallam* divided the work between Ali *radhiAllahu 'anhu*, who worked outside of the house, and Fatima *radhiAllahu 'anha,* who took care of the house. At one point, Fatima *radhiAllahu 'anha* asked the Prophet *sallAllahu 'alayhi wa sallam* for a servant because her hands were getting worn from the housework.

Ali *radhiAllahu 'anhu* narrated, *"Fatima radhiAllahu 'anha complained of what she suffered from the hand mill and from grinding, when she got the news that some slave girls of the booty had been brought to Allah's Messenger sallAllahu 'alayhi wa sallam. She went to him to ask for a maid-servant, but she could not find him, and told 'Aisha of her need. When the Prophet sallAllahu 'alayhi wa sallam came, 'Aisha informed him of that. The Prophet sallAllahu 'alayhi wa sallam came to our house when we had gone to our beds. (On seeing the Prophet) we were going to get up, but he said, 'Keep at your places,' I felt the coolness of the Prophet's feet on my chest. Then he said, "Shall I tell you a thing which is better than what you asked me for? When you go to your beds, say: Allahu Akbar (Allah is Greater) for 34 times, and Alhamdulillah (All the praises are for Allah) for 33 times, and SubhanAllah (Glorified be Allah) for 33 times. This is better for you than what you have requested."*

Other scholars say it is preferred for women to do household chores. However, based on the same reasoning and *hadith* that have been mentioned, if the husband is working outside of the home, then it becomes obligatory on the wife to take care of household tasks. Yet others say it becomes obligatory if the husband asks her to the household work based upon the *hadith, "If I was to order anyone to make sujood to another it would be a wife to her husband."*

Some scholars say the issue of women managing household chores depends on the custom of her society. While the scholars differ on this issue, it seems the more prevalent opinion is that the woman should manage the household chores. This is because of the two *hadiths* mentioned above and the custom at the time of the Prophet *sallAllahu 'alayhi wa sallam* and afterwards in most societies.

---

187. Sahih Al-Bukhari

Made in the USA
Middletown, DE
19 September 2024

61063117R00075